Framework 7

MATHS A

Ray Allan

Martin Williams

Claire Perry

OXFORD

UNIVERSITY PRESS

OXFORD
UNIVERSITY PRESS

Great Clarendon Street, Oxford OX2 6DP

Oxford University Press is a department of the University of Oxford.
It furthers the University's objective of excellence in research,
scholarship, and education by publishing worldwide in

Oxford New York

Auckland Bangkok Buenos Aires Cape Town Chennai
Dar es Salaam Delhi Hong Kong Istanbul Karachi Kolkata
Kuala Lumpur Madrid Melbourne Mexico City Mumbai Nairobi
São Paulo Shanghai Taipei Tokyo Toronto

Oxford is a registered trade mark of Oxford University Press
in the UK and in certain other countries

British Library Cataloguing in Publication Data

Data available

ISBN 019 914 939 9

10 9 8 7 6 5 4 3 2

Typeset by Mathematical Composition Setters Ltd.

Printed in Italy by Rotolito Lombarda

Acknowledgements

The photograph on the cover is reproduced courtesy of Pictor International
(UK).

The publisher and authors would like to thank the following for permission
to use photographs and other copyright material:

Alamy Images: p 15; Corbis/Ed Bock: p 157; Corbis/Ralph A Clevenger: p 235;
Corbis/David Pollack: p 220; Corbis/Royalty Free: p 244; Corel Professional
Photos: p 69 (top left); Empics: pp 29, 100; Getty Images/Photographers
Choice: p 221; Ingram Publishing: p 69 (bottom left & right); Oxford
University Press: pp 134, 155, 190; Photodisc: pp 1, 69 (top right), 131, 182;
Martin Sookias: p 181.

Cover image is by Pictor.

Figurative artwork is by Paul Daviz

About this book

This book has been specifically written for students who have gained Level 2 or 3 at the end of KS2. It is designed to help students consolidate their achievement at Level 3. The content is designed to provide access to the Support Book in the same series and the two books can be used along side each other in the classroom.

The authors are experienced teachers who have been working with students of a similar ability for years and so are well qualified to provide appropriate classroom practice.

The book is made up of units that provide access to the Support tier of the sample medium term plans that complement the Framework for Teaching Mathematics at KS3.

The units are:

A1	Sequences	1–14
N1	Number calculations	15–28
S1	Perimeter and area	29–38
N2	Fractions, decimals and percentages	39–52
D1	Data and probability	53–66
A2	Using symbols	67–78
S2	Angles and shapes	79–86
D2	Handling data	87–98
N3	Multiplication and division	99–116
A3	Functions and graphs	117–130
S3	Triangles and quadrilaterals	131–142
N4	Percentages, ratio and proportion	143–154
A4	Linear equations	155–164
S4	Transformations	165–178
N5	More number calculations	179–196
D3	The handling data cycle	197–208
D4	Probability experiments	209–216
A5	Equations and graphs	217–234
S5	Angles and symmetry	235–248

Each unit comprises double page spreads that should take a lesson to teach. These are shown on the full contents list.

Problem solving is integrated throughout the material as suggested in the Framework.

How to use this book

This book is made up of units of work which are colour coded into: Algebra (Blue), Data (Pink), Number (Orange), Shape, space and measures (Green).

Each unit of work starts with an overview of the content of the unit, as specified in the Primary Framework document, so that you know exactly what you are expected to learn.

This unit will show you how to:

▶▶ Recognise and extend number sequences.

▶▶ Recognise odd and even numbers.

▶▶ Understand doing and undoing operations.

▶▶ Know multiplications up to 5 × 10 and work out similar divisions.

▶▶ Solve mathematical problems and puzzles.

▶▶ Recognise and describe patterns.

The first page of a unit also highlights the skills and facts you should already know and provides Check in questions to help you revise before you start so that you are ready to apply the knowledge later in the unit:

Before you start

You should know how to ...

1 Count on or back in steps.

2 Recognise odd and even numbers.

Check in

1 For each question, continue for six steps.

   a Count on from 2 in steps of 3.

    Write: 2, _, _, _, _, _

   b Count back from 30 in steps of 4.

    Write: 30, _, _, _, _, _

2 Write the odd numbers from this list:

| 9 | 16 | 25 | 36 | 100 | 312 |

Inside each unit, the content develops in double page spreads which all follow the same structure.

The spreads start with a list of the learning outcomes and a summary of the keywords:

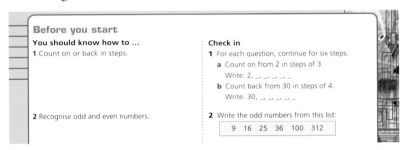

This spread will show you how to:

▶ Calculate the perimeter and area of simple shapes.

▶ Use the formula in words for the area of a rectangle.

KEYWORDS

Perimeter   Area

Edge   Surface

Length   Rectangle

The keywords are summarised and defined in a Glossary at the end of the book so you can always check what they mean.

Key information is highlighted in the text so you can see the facts you need to learn.

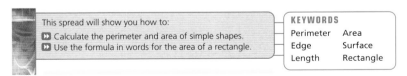

▶ To multiply by 4, you double the 2 times table.

Examples showing the key skills and techniques you need to develop are shown in boxes. Also hint boxes show tips and reminders you may find useful:

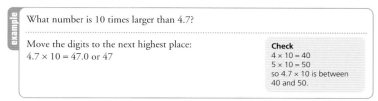

What number is 10 times larger than 4.7?

Move the digits to the next highest place:
$4.7 \times 10 = 47.0$ or 47

Check
$4 \times 10 = 40$
$5 \times 10 = 50$
so 4.7×10 is between 40 and 50.

Each exercise is carefully graded, set at three levels of difficulty:

1. The first few questions provide lead-in questions, revising previous learning.
2. The questions in the middle of the exercise provide the main focus of the material.
3. The last few questions are challenging questions that provide a link to the Support tier learning objectives.

At the end of each unit is a summary page so that you can revise the learning of the unit before moving on.

Check out questions are provided to help you check your understanding of the key concepts covered and your ability to apply the key techniques.

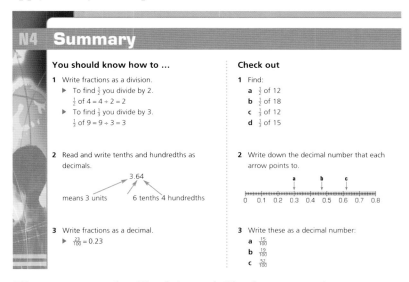

N4 Summary

You should know how to ...

1 Write fractions as a division.
  ▶ To find $\frac{1}{2}$ you divide by 2.
    $\frac{1}{2}$ of $4 = 4 \div 2 = 2$
  ▶ To find $\frac{1}{3}$ you divide by 3.
    $\frac{1}{3}$ of $9 = 9 \div 3 = 3$

2 Read and write tenths and hundredths as decimals.

    3.64

    means 3 units   6 tenths 4 hundredths

3 Write fractions as a decimal.
  ▶ $\frac{23}{100} = 0.23$

Check out

1 Find:
  a $\frac{1}{2}$ of 12
  b $\frac{1}{2}$ of 18
  c $\frac{1}{3}$ of 12
  d $\frac{1}{3}$ of 15

2 Write down the decimal number that each arrow points to.

    0   0.1 0.2 0.3 0.4 0.5 0.6 0.7 0.8

3 Write these as a decimal number:
  a $\frac{15}{100}$
  b $\frac{19}{100}$
  c $\frac{52}{100}$

The answers to the Check in and Check out questions are produced at the end of the book so that you can check your own progress and identify any areas that need work.

Contents

A1 Sequences   1–14

A1.1	Patterns	2
A1.2	Introducing sequences	4
A1.3	Sequences and rules	6
A1.4	Sequences in diagrams	8
A1.5	Doing and undoing	10
A1.6	Operation machines	12
	Summary	14

N1 Number calculations   15–28

N1.1	Place value	16
N1.2	Negative numbers	18
N1.3	Adding and subtracting with negatives	20
N1.4	Mental addition	22
N1.5	Mental subtraction	24
N1.6	Multiplying by 10	26
	Summary	28

S1 Perimeter and area   29–38

S1.1	Measurements and scales	30
S1.2	Perimeter	32
S1.3	Area	34
S1.4	Perimeter and area	36
	Summary	38

N2 Fractions, decimals and percentages   39–52

N2.1	Understanding fractions	40
N2.2	Comparing fractions	42
N2.3	Fractions of amounts	44
N2.4	Decimal scales	46
N2.5	Decimals and percentages	48
N2.6	Finding tenths of amounts	50
	Summary	52

D1 Data and probability   53–66
D1.1   The mode   54
D1.2   What's in the middle?   56
D1.3   Levelling   58
D1.4   Introducing chance   60
D1.5   Describing chance   62
D1.6   The probability scale   64
    Summary   66

A2 Using symbols   67–78
A2.1   Using letters   68
A2.2   Adding and subtracting with symbols   70
A2.3   Solving algebra problems   72
A2.4   Symbols and values   74
A2.5   Substitution   76
    Summary   78

S2 Angles and shapes   79–86
S2.1   Time   80
S2.2   Reading coordinates   82
S2.3   Coordinates and shapes   84
    Summary   86

D2 Handling data   87–98
D2.1   Sorting   88
D2.2   Reading diagrams   90
D2.3   Organising data   92
D2.4   Displaying data   94
D2.5   Interpreting data   96
    Summary   98

N3 Multiplication and division   99–116

N3.1	Rounding numbers	100
N3.2	Mental multiplication	102
N3.3	Multiplying decimals by 10	104
N3.4	Dividing whole numbers by 10	106
N3.5	Number and measure	108
N3.6	Multiplying by partitioning	110
N3.7	Division on a number line	112
N3.8	More division ideas	114
	Summary	116

A3 Functions and graphs   117–130

A3.1	Factors	118
A3.2	Multiples	120
A3.3	Square numbers	122
A3.4	Multiplication mappings	124
A3.5	Plotting pairs	126
A3.6	Mappings and graphs	128
	Summary	130

S3 Triangles and quadrilaterals   131–142

S3.1	Compass turns	132
S3.2	Angles	134
S3.3	Measuring angles	136
S3.4	Drawing angles	138
S3.5	Parallel and perpendicular lines	140
	Summary	142

N4 Percentages, ratio and proportion   143–154

N4.1	Fractions	144
N4.2	Fractions and decimals	146
N4.3	Fractions, decimals and percentages	148
N4.4	Percentages of amounts	150
N4.5	Ratio	152
	Summary	154

A4 Linear equations   155–164
  A4.1 Using letters   156
  A4.2 Equalities   158
  A4.3 Inequalities   160
  A4.4 Equations   162
       Summary   164

S4 Transformations   165–178
  S4.1 Symmetry   166
  S4.2 Reflection symmetry   168
  S4.3 Symmetry on a grid   170
  S4.4 Translating shapes   172
  S4.5 Rotation   174
  S4.6 Movement on a grid   176
       Summary   178

N5 More number calculations   179–196
  N5.1 Estimating   180
  N5.2 Approximations   182
  N5.3 Using factors   184
  N5.4 Written calculations   186
  N5.5 Written division   188
  N5.6 Equivalent fractions   190
  N5.7 Finding fractions of amounts   192
  N5.8 Finding percentages   194
       Summary   196

D3 The handling data cycle   197–208
  D3.1 Collecting data   198
  D3.2 Drawing pictograms   200
  D3.3 Drawing charts and graphs   202
  D3.4 Using statistics   204
  D3.5 Discussing findings   206
       Summary   208

D4 Probability experiments   209–216

   D4.1   Describing probabilities   210
   D4.2   A probability experiment   212
   D4.3   More experiments   214
           Summary   216

A5 Equations and graphs   217–234

   A5.1   Solving equations   218
   A5.2   Using formulas   220
   A5.3   Using symbols in formulas   222
   A5.4   Making sequences   224
   A5.5   Rules   226
   A5.6   Rules and graphs   228
   A5.7   Graphs of formulas   230
   A5.8   Coordinates in all quadrants   232
           Summary   234

S5 Angles and symmetry   235–248

   S5.1   Angle facts   236
   S5.2   Triangles and quadrilaterals   238
   S5.3   Solid shapes   240
   S5.4   Line symmetry   242
   S5.5   Rotational symmetry   244
   S5.6   Tessellations   246
           Summary   248

Glossary   249
Check in and check out answers   264
Index   274

1 Sequences

This unit will show you how to:

▶▶ Recognise and extend number sequences.

▶▶ Recognise odd and even numbers.

▶▶ Understand doing and undoing operations.

▶▶ Know multiplications up to 5×10 and work out similar divisions.

▶▶ Solve mathematical problems and puzzles.

▶▶ Recognise and describe patterns.

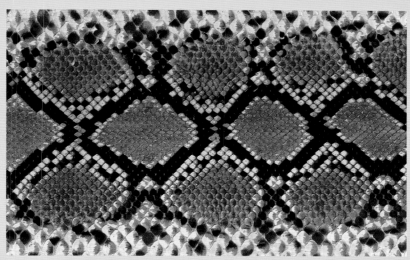

Many animals have patterns on their skin.

Before you start

You should know how to ...

1 Count on or back in steps.

2 Recognise odd and even numbers.

3 Know addition and subtraction facts for each number up to 20.

Check in

1 For each question, continue for six steps.

   a Count on from 2 in steps of 3.

     Write: 2, _, _, _, _, _

   b Count back from 30 in steps of 4.

     Write: 30, _, _, _, _, _

2 Write the odd numbers from this list:

| 9 | 16 | 25 | 36 | 100 | 312 |

3 Find the missing number in each of these sums:

   a $8 + ? = 20$ **b** $? + 17 = 20$

   c $20 - ? = 11$ **d** $20 - ? = 7$

   e $? - 6 = 14$ **f** $? + 4 = 20$

This spread will show you how to:

▶▶ Recognise and extend number sequences.

KEYWORDS
Pattern   Increase
Sequence   Repeat

Patterns are all around you:

Bricks in a wall ...

decoration on a plate ...

pattern on a school tie

Claire is drawing a pattern.

She repeats the shape.

Claire is putting coloured beads on a string in a sequence:
red, then yellow, then blue.

She repeats the sequence:

These patterns grow instead of repeating:

The number of squares increases by 2 each time.

2 squares   4 squares   6 squares

The number of dots increases by 4 each time.

4 dots   8 dots   12 dots

Exercise A1.1

1 Which part of these patterns is missing?
Is it **x**, **y** or **z**?

a
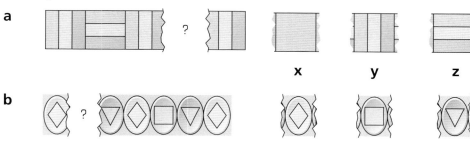

b

2 Copy this pattern on to squared paper.
Continue the pattern five more times.

This is the pattern

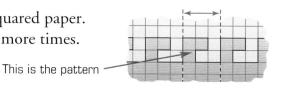

3 What is the colour of the next bead in each of these patterns?

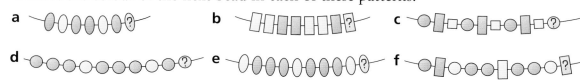

a   **b**   **c**

d   **e**   **f**

4 These cards show a sequence that repeats.
What is the next card in each sequence?

a   **b**

5 Find the next number in each sequence pattern.

a
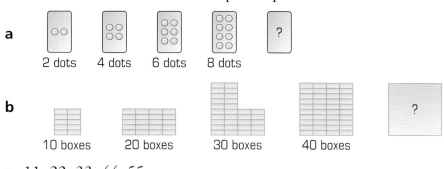

2 dots   4 dots   6 dots   8 dots

b

10 boxes   20 boxes   30 boxes   40 boxes

c 11, 22, 33, 44, 55, ____

This spread will show you how to:

▶▶ Recognise and extend number sequences.

KEYWORDS
Sequence   Order
Rule

When numbers follow a pattern or rule they are in a sequence.

The house numbers in this street are a sequence.

The sequence of house numbers starts at 2.   The last number in the sequence is 10.

The numbers on these locker doors make a sequence.

This sequence starts with the number 25. You take away 5 to find the next number.

The rule is −5.

The last locker is 10 − 5 = 5.

You can continue a sequence by following the rule.

example

Write the first four numbers in each sequence.

a Start at 3 with rule +4   **b** Start at 13 with rule −2

....

a   3,   7,   11,   15
           +4   +4   +4

b   13,   11,   9,   7
           −2   −2   −2

You write a comma between each number.

Exercise A1.2

1 Jack is on his 'Space Hopper'. He is bouncing along a number line.

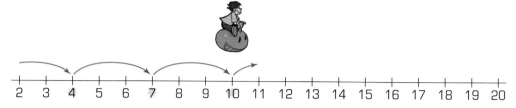

   a What is the next number Jack will land on? What is the rule?

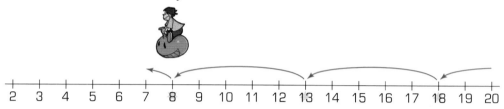

   b What is the next number Jack will land on? What is the rule?

2 What is the next number in each sequence?
   a 2, 4, 6, 8, ____   **b** 1, 4, 7, 10, ____
   c 3, 5, 7, 9, ____   **d** 2, 6, 10, 14, ____
   e 5, 10, 15, 20, ____   **f** 10, 20, 30, 40, ____
   g 9, 7, 5, 3, ____   **h** 15, 12, 9, 6, ____
   i 20, 16, 12, 8, ____   **j** 60, 50, 40, 30, ____

3 Write the first four numbers in each sequence using the rule.
   The first one is done for you.
   a The first number is 2. The rule is +4.
   b The first number is 5. The rule is +3.
   c The first number is 21. The rule is −3.
   d The first number is 50. The rule is −10.
   e The first number is 11. The rule is +5.
   f The first number is 24. The rule is −4.

> Your answer will look like this:
> **a** 2, 6, 10, 14

4 Brain teaser
   These are the numbers in a sequence: 11, 5, 9, 3, 7
   a Write the numbers out in order – the first number will be 3.
   b What is the rule?
   c What will the sixth number be?

This spread will show you how to:

▶▶ Recognise and extend number sequences.

KEYWORDS
Rule   Term
Sequence   Difference

Amy describes a rule to Meara.
Meara cannot work out the sequence.

Amy tells Meara the first number.
Now Meara knows where to start.

▶ To describe a sequence, you need a start number and a rule.

example

Describe this sequence using a rule:
2, 5, 8, 11, 14, ...

The dots mean that the sequence goes on for ever.

The sequence starts at 2 and goes up in threes.
The rule is +3.

▶ Each number in a sequence is called a term:

9,   13,   17,   21

The first term   The second term   The third term   The fourth term

To find the rule, you work out the difference between each term.

example

Find the next two terms in each sequence.

a 3, 7, 11, 15, __, __

b 20, 17, 14, 11, __, __

a 3   7   11   15
          +4   +4   +4

The difference between each term
is +4: The rule is +4.
The next two terms are:
19 and 23.

b 20   17   14   11
            −3   −3   −3

The difference between each term
is −3: The rule is −3.
The next two terms are:
8 and 5.

Exercise A1.3

1 Amy describes some sequences.
Write out the first five terms for each sequence.
  a Start at 4. The rule is +5.
  b Start at 23. The rule is -3.
  c Start at 0. The rule is +4.
  d Start at 21. The rule is -4.
  e Start at 30. The rule is +2.

2 Copy and complete this description for each of these sequences:

> Start at _____ . The rule is _____ .

  a 1, 4, 7, 10, ...   **b** 17, 14, 11, 8, ...
  c 9, 13, 17, 21, ...   **d** 80, 70, 60, 50, ...
  e 29, 24, 19, 14, ...   **f** 8, 15, 22, 29, ...

3 Copy and complete these statements for each of the sequences.

> ▸ The first term is _____.
> ▸ The difference between each term is _____.
> ▸ The rule is _____.
> ▸ The next three terms are _____, _____, _____.

  a 2, 5, 8, 11, ...   **b** 2, 3, 4, 5, ...
  c 20, 18, 16, 14, 12, ...   **d** 5, 7, 9, 11, 13, ...
  e 2, 10, 18, 26, ...   **f** 3, 6, 9, 12, 15, ...
  g 30, 26, 22, 18, 14, ...   **h** 20, 30, 40, 50, ...

4 Brain teaser
  a Work out the two missing terms in this sequence.
    4, __, 10, __, 16

  b The third term in this sequence is 11.
    The rule is +3.
    Write out the sequence.

    __, __, 11, __, __

Sequences in diagrams

This spread will show you how to:
▶▶ Recognise odd and even numbers and their properties.

KEYWORDS
Rule   Sequence
Odd   Even

Andy and Sara are building a bench.
They find out why odd numbers are called odd numbers.

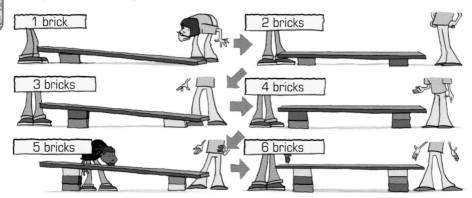

1 brick → 2 bricks
3 bricks → 4 bricks
5 bricks → 6 bricks

Even numbers can be divided exactly by 2.
You can show other number sequences using picture patterns.

example

Use multilink cubes to describe this number sequence:
3, 5, 7, 9, ...

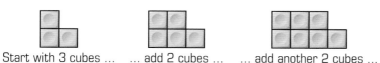

Start with 3 cubes ...   ... add 2 cubes ...   ... add another 2 cubes ...   ... and another 2.

The first term is 3. The rule is add 2.

▶ You can describe patterns using number sequences.

example

Describe this sequence in words.

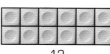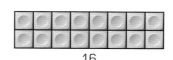

4   8   12   16

The first term is 4.
You add 4 cubes each time, so the rule is +4.
This is the pattern for the 4 times table.

The sequence contains even numbers only.

Exercise A1.4

1 a Copy and complete the sequence of odd numbers up to 15.
1, 3, 5, ___, ___, ___, ___, 15

b Copy and complete the sequence of even numbers up to 20.
2, 4, 6, ___, ___, ___, ___, ___, ___, 20

2 Is the next number in these sequences odd or even?
a 4, 8, 12, 16, __   **b** 1, 3, 5, 7, 9, __

3 This diagram shows the 2 times table.

    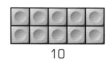
2   4   6   8   10

Diagrams **a**, **b** and **c** show the 3 times, 4 times and 5 times tables.
Some parts of the diagrams are missing.
Complete each pattern by choosing the missing part from the box.

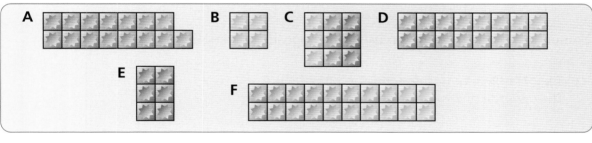

4 a Copy and complete this grid.
There are nine sequences within the grid, four across the page, four down and one diagonal (corner to corner).
b Write out each of the nine sequences.
c How many of the sequences have only even number terms?

2	4	6	?
3	6	?	?
?	8	12	?
5	?	?	?

This spread will show you how to:

▶▶ Understand doing and undoing operations.

KEYWORDS
Opposite   Add
Operation   Multiply
Divide   Take away

Many actions can be undone, or reversed.

The action:
Harry walked up five steps.
He turned the light on, and
entered the bathroom.

Undoing the action:
Harry left the bathroom
and turned the light off.
He walked down five steps.

You undo a number operation using the opposite operation.

▶ The opposite of + is −, and the opposite of − is +.
The opposite of × is ÷, and the opposite of ÷ is ×.

To undo the operation + 2
use the opposite, − 2

```
          ┌── undo operation ──┐
                               ↓
4 + 2 = 6   ──────→   6 − 2 = 4
```

To undo the operation × 4
use the opposite, ÷ 4

```
          ┌── undo operation ──┐
                               ↓
3 × 4 = 12  ──────→   12 ÷ 4 = 3
```

To undo the operation − 3
use the opposite, + 3

```
          ┌── undo operation ──┐
                               ↓
7 − 3 = 4   ──────→   4 + 3 = 7
```

To undo the operation ÷ 2
use the opposite, × 2

```
          ┌── undo operation ──┐
                               ↓
8 ÷ 2 = 4   ──────→   4 × 2 = 8
```

Exercise A1.5

1 Write out the opposite to each action.
- **a** Turn a tap on.
- **b** Stand up.
- **c** Open your eyes.
- **d** Drive downhill.
- **e** Breathe in.
- **f** Put your shoes on.
- **g** Climb up a ladder.
- **h** Shut the door.

2 Re-write this story so that Joe will 'undo' all of the actions.
The story is started for you.

> Joe opened his bag.
> He took his pen from the bag and then took out his book.
> He sat down.
> He opened the book, and breathed in.
> He fell asleep.

Write: *Joe woke up. He breathed out and ...*

3 Each question shows an operation.
Find the correct opposite operation from the list.

a

b
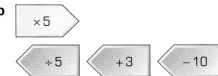

c
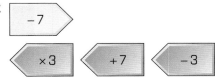

d

4 Copy and complete these questions by finding the opposite operation.
- **a** $4 + 6 = 10 \rightarrow 10 - \underline{\quad} = 4$
- **b** $9 - 5 = 4 \rightarrow 4 + \underline{\quad} = 9$
- **c** $13 + 4 = 17 \rightarrow 17 - \underline{\quad} = 13$
- **d** $12 - 4 = 8 \rightarrow 8 + \underline{\quad} = 12$
- **e** $5 \times 3 = 15 \rightarrow 15 \div \underline{\quad} = 5$
- **f** $10 \div 2 = 5 \rightarrow 5 \times \underline{\quad} = 10$
- **g** $10 \times 4 = 40 \rightarrow 40 \,\square\, 4 = 10$
- **h** $12 \div 4 = 3 \rightarrow 3 \,\square\, 4 = 12$

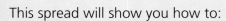

This spread will show you how to:

▶▶ Know multiplications up to 5 × 10 and work out similar divisions.

KEYWORDS
Operation   Output
Multiply   Machine
Input

Harry works for five days each week.
His bus fares cost £3 each day.

Harry uses a calculator to work out the cost of travel.

> ▶ He **inputs** the number of days (5) and multiplies by 3.
> ▶ The calculator **outputs** the answer.
> ▶ The cost is £15.

You can show this calculation using a machine.

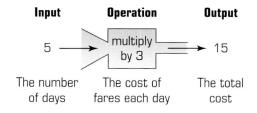

```
Input          Operation          Output

5  ──────▶   multiply  ──────▶    15
              by 3

The number    The cost of        The total
of days       fares each day     cost
```

To find the cost of fares for 10 days, change the input to 10.

```
Input          Operation          Output

10 ──────▶      × 3    ──────▶    30
```

The output shows the cost is £30.

The bus company has a Special Offer.

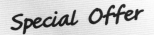

Special Offer
**Pay all your fares
at the start of the week.
We'll give you £2 back!**

The machine contains two operations:

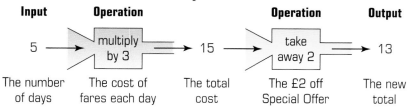

```
Input        Operation              Operation       Output

5  ────▶  multiply  ──▶ 15 ──▶      take    ──────▶ 13
           by 3                     away 2

The number   The cost of   The total   The £2 off        The new
of days      fares each day cost       Special Offer     total
```

Exercise A1.6

1 Find the output for each of these machines.

a  3 → add 4 → Output

b  4 → multiply by 3 → Output

c 7 → +9 → Output

d 3 → ×10 → Output

2 Find the output for each machine when the input is 6.

a  +3

b   −4

c 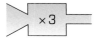 ×3

d   ÷2

3 These machines contain two operations.
Find the outputs from the given inputs. The first one is done for you.

a 5 → ×2 → +1 → 11

5   × 2 = 10 → 10 + 1   =   11

b  2 → ×3 → +2 → Output

c 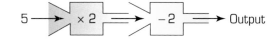 5 → ×2 → −2 → Output

d 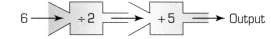 6 → ÷2 → +5 → Output

e  3 → +7 → ×2 → Output

4 Brain teaser
What could the operation be for each of these machines?

a 3 → ? → 7

b 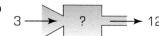 3 → ? → 12

13

You should know how to ...

1 Recognise and extend number sequences.

▶ In the sequence:

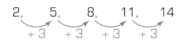

2,   5,   8,   11,   14
 +3   +3   +3   +3

you start at 2 and add on 3.

2 Know multiplications to 5 × 10 and work out similar divisions.

Remember:
 4 × 8 = 32
so 32 ÷ 8 = 4

Check out

1 a What are the next two numbers in this sequence?

18, 21, 24, 27

b Find the missing numbers in this sequence.

__, __, 23, 27, __, 34, 37, __

Explain the rule

2 a Write down the answers to:

3 × 7 =

4 × 9 =

8 × 6 =

b Find the answers to:

21 ÷ 3 =

36 ÷ 9 =

48 ÷ 8 =

c Work out the answers to:

30 × 7 =

360 ÷ 9 =

60 × 8 =

Number calculations

This unit will show you how to:

▶▶ Partition numbers into 1000s, 100s, 10s and 1s.

▶▶ Understand the decimal point and place value.

▶▶ Use symbols correctly.

▶▶ Know addition and subtraction facts to 20.

▶▶ Partition into tens and units, adding up the tens first.

▶▶ Use place value to add or subtract mentally.

▶▶ Multiply any whole number by 10.

▶▶ Use a calculator.

▶▶ Recognise negative numbers in context.

▶▶ Order a set of positive and negative whole numbers.

▶▶ Calculate a temperature rise and fall across 0°C.

▶▶ Choose and use appropriate ways of calculating to solve problems.

You use negative numbers to describe freezing temperatures!

Before you start

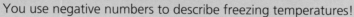

You should know how to …

1 Read and write whole numbers in words.

2 Order whole numbers.

3 Find a difference by counting on.

Check in

1 a Write this number in words:
374.

   b Write this number using digits:
four hundred and twenty-three.

2 Order these numbers.
Use a number line to help you.
   a 35   17   26   23   41
   b 170   203   89   325   142

3 Find the difference between each of these pairs of numbers:
   a 3 and 10   **b** 17 and 21   **c** 83 and 68.

This spread will show you how to:

▶▶ Partition numbers into 1000s, 100s, 10s and 1s.
▶▶ Understand the decimal point and place value.
▶▶ Use symbols correctly.

KEYWORDS

Digit	Decimal
Hundreds	Tenths
Tens	Place value
Units	Interval

In this ring:

▶ The pink shapes have a value of 100.
▶ The yellow shapes have a value of 10.
▶ The green shapes have a value of 1.

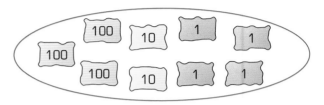

The value of the numbers in the ring is:

$$3 \times 100 \ (= 300) \qquad 2 \times 10 \ (= 20) \qquad \text{and } 4 \times 1 \ (= 4).$$

324

To show the number 431 you need:

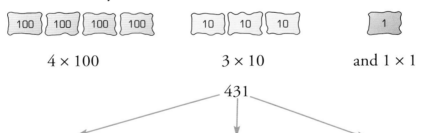

4×100 3×10 and 1×1

431

The digit 4 is in the 100s place so it has a value of 400.

The digit 3 is in the 10s place so it has a value of 30.

The digit 1 is in the 1s place so it has a value of 1.

This arrow is pointing to a position between 3 and 4.

You can divide the interval between 3 and 4 into ten equal parts.
Each part is a tenth.

The position of the arrow is at **3.6**.

3 whole units and 6 tenths.

The arrow is 6 tenths from 3.

Exercise N1.1

1 What is the value of each of these groups of shapes?

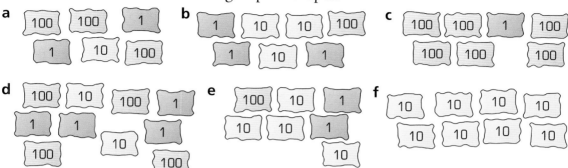

2 Use shapes like the ones in question 1 to show these numbers.
   a 215   **b** 304   **c** 40   **d** 202   **e** 512   **f** 34

3 In the number 432:
   ▸ the digit 4 has a value of 400
   ▸ the digit 3 has a value of 30
   ▸ the digit 2 has a value of 2.

Choose a number from the ring which has a:
   a 4 digit with a value of 40
   b 5 digit with a value of 500
   c 1 digit with a value of 1.

4 What is the position of the arrow on each of these number lines?

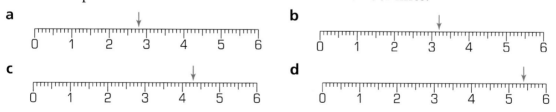

5 Use the number lines in question 4 to decide which number
   in each pair is bigger.

> means 'is bigger than'.   < means 'is smaller than'.

The first two are done for you.
   a 3.0 < 3.2   **b** 4.1 > 3.9   **c** 5.3, 3.9   **d** 5.2, 4.1
   e 3.8, 1.0   **f** 1.7, 7.0   **g** 0.5, 0.2   **h** 2.3, 1.6

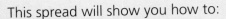

This spread will show you how to:

▶▶ Recognise negative numbers in context.
▶▶ Order a set of positive and negative whole numbers.

KEYWORDS

Negative   Minus
Positive   Zero
Increase   Decrease
Temperature

You can measure temperatures in degrees Celsius or °C.

On a thermometer:

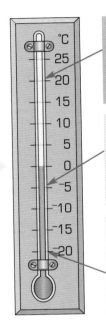

Temperatures higher than 0 °C are positive.

The numbers change from positive to negative at zero.

Temperatures below 0 °C are negative.

Your classroom should be at about 20 °C.

You use a minus or negative symbol below 0°C: ⁻5 °C is 5° below zero.

You would be much too cold if the temperature was ⁻20 °C.

As the temperature increases it becomes warmer:
1 °C is warmer than ⁻5 °C.

> The red arrow shows the increase in temperature.
> Start at ⁻5 °C and count until you get to 1 °C.
> You should count 6°.

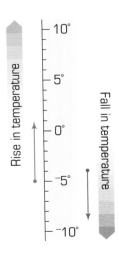

As the temperature decreases it becomes colder:
⁻9 °C is colder than ⁻4 °C.

> The blue arrow shows the decrease in temperature
> Start at ⁻4 °C and count until you reach ⁻9 °C.
> You should count 5°.

Exercise N1.2

1 Write the temperature marked on each of these thermometers.
Use the minus sign for negative numbers, like this: ⁻6°.

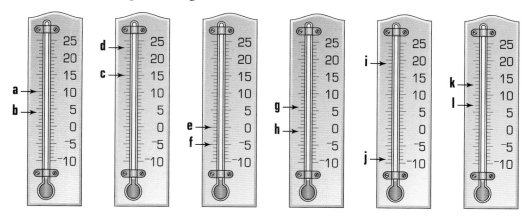

2 On the thermometer scale, ⁻5° is lower than ⁻2°.
Which is the lower temperature in each of these pairs?
a ⁻6° or ⁻2°   **b** ⁻3° or ⁻4°   **c** ⁻1° or ⁻10°   **d** 2° or ⁻2°
e 8° or ⁻10°   **f** ⁻7° or 6°   **g** 3° or 7°   **h** 0° or 5°

3 Use the correct sign to link these pairs of temperatures.

> > means 'is bigger than'.   < means 'is smaller than'.

For example: 3° > ⁻1° means 3° is bigger than ⁻1°
⁻5° < 2° means ⁻5° is smaller than 2°

a ⁻6°   3°   **b** ⁻7°   ⁻2°   **c** ⁻9°   5°   **d** 8°   0°

4 The three dots on the thermometer show these temperatures:
2°, ⁻1°, ⁻5°.
In size order the temperatures are: ⁻5°, ⁻1°, 2°.
Put these temperatures in order, starting with the lowest.
a ⁻9°, ⁻3°, ⁻5°   **b** ⁻1°, ⁻3°, ⁻2°   **c** 0°, ⁻7°, ⁻5°
d ⁻8°, 0°, ⁻10°   **e** 5°, ⁻10°, ⁻6°   **f** 4°, 9°, ⁻9°

5 These are typical winter temperatures of some cities.
London: 8°   Moscow: ⁻6°   Bangkok: 32°   Montreal: ⁻9°
a Which is the coldest city?
b Which is the warmest city?
c Which cities have a typical winter temperature above zero?

This spread will show you how to:

▶▶ Calculate a temperature rise or fall across 0 °C.

KEYWORDS

Increase   Add

Decrease   Subtract

Positive   Negative

This is a horizontal thermometer.

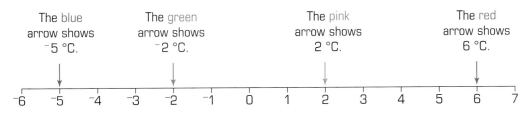

The blue arrow shows ⁻5 °C.

The green arrow shows ⁻2 °C.

The pink arrow shows 2 °C.

The red arrow shows 6 °C.

▶ On a horizontal thermometer, you move to the right to get warmer.

example

The temperature in Brighton one night is ⁻2 °C.
The next day it rises by 5 °C.
What is the daytime temperature?

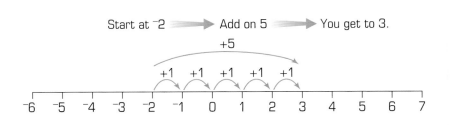

Start at ⁻2 ⟹ Add on 5 ⟹ You get to 3.

▶ You move to the left to get colder.

The difference between 4 °C and ⁻3 °C is 7 °C:

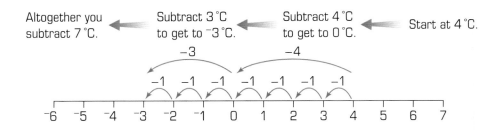

Altogether you subtract 7 °C. ⟵ Subtract 3 °C to get to ⁻3 °C. ⟵ Subtract 4 °C to get to 0 °C. ⟵ Start at 4 °C.

▶ You **subtract** to find the difference between two temperatures.

Exercise N1.3

1 What are the positions of the arrows on this thermometer?

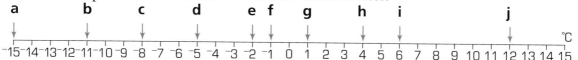

2 Use this thermometer to help you answer the questions.

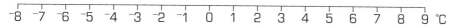

What temperature is:
a 1 °C warmer than ⁻1 °C
b 4 °C warmer than ⁻4 °C
c 6 °C warmer than ⁻6 °C
d 9 °C warmer than ⁻9 °C
e 7 °C colder than 0 °C
f 12 °C colder than 0 °C?

3 Copy and complete these temperature calculations.
Some of your answers will be negative numbers, write them carefully.

The temperature is ⁻2 °C. What is the new temperature after it:
a rises by 6 °C   **b** rises by 8 °C   **c** rises by 4 °C
d rises by 9 °C   **e** rises by 3 °C   **f** rises by 7 °C
g falls by 6 °C   **h** falls by 1 °C   **i** falls by 7 °C

4 Calculate the difference between each pair of temperatures.
a 2 °C and ⁻5 °C   **b** 3 °C and ⁻1 °C   **c** ⁻7 °C and 0 °C
d ⁻5 °C and 10 °C   **e** 4 °C and ⁻4 °C   **f** ⁻3 °C and 5 °C
g ⁻5 °C and ⁻1 °C   **h** ⁻4 °C and ⁻7 °C   **i** ⁻8 °C and ⁻1 °C

5 If the temperature starts at 3 °C and stops at ⁻2 °C it has fallen by 5 °C.
You write 3 °C − 5 °C = ⁻2 °C.
Work out the rise or fall in temperature for each question.
Say clearly whether it has risen or fallen.
a Start at 4 °C and stop at ⁻3 °C   **b** Start at ⁻2 °C and stop at 5 °C
c Start at 1 °C and stop at ⁻8 °C   **d** Start at 2 °C and stop at ⁻5 °C
e Start at ⁻8 °C and stop at 0 °C   **f** Start at ⁻7 °C and stop at ⁻1 °C

This spread will show you how to:

▶▶ Know addition and subtraction facts to 20.
▶▶ Partition into tens and units.
▶▶ Use place value to add mentally.

KEYWORDS

Addition   Pair
Calculation   Add
Number line

These pairs of numbers add up to 20.

0	1	2	3	4	5	6	7	8	9	10	11	12	13	14	15	16	17	18	19	20
20	19	18	17	16	15	14	13	12	11	10	9	8	7	6	5	4	3	2	1	0

You can use these facts to work out calculations quickly in your head.

You can use a number line for other calculations.

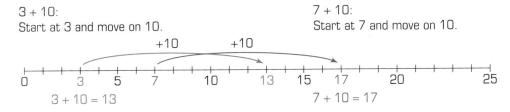

3 + 10:
Start at 3 and move on 10.

7 + 10:
Start at 7 and move on 10.

3 + 10 = 13

7 + 10 = 17

▶ There is a pattern:
When you add 10, you add a 1 to the **tens** place.

You can use a number line to add larger numbers: 15 + 30 = 45.

Start with a blank line.

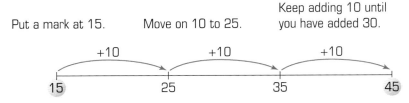

Put a mark at 15.   Move on 10 to 25.   Keep adding 10 until you have added 30.

A number line can help with more difficult additions: 15 + 33 = 48.

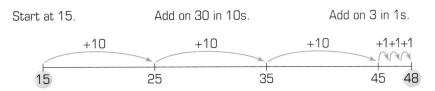

Start at 15.   Add on 30 in 10s.   Add on 3 in 1s.

Exercise N1.6

1 Multiply these numbers by 10.
Do as many as you can in one minute.
a 3 **b** 5 **c** 8 **d** 1 **e** 7 **f** 4 **g** 6 **h** 9 **i** 2

2 Multiply these numbers by 10.
Move all the digits to the next highest place.
a 16 **b** 13 **c** 17 **d** 12 **e** 15 **f** 19 **g** 14

3 These pipes are each 10 metres long.
Two pipes joined together measure 2 × 10 m = 20 m.

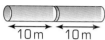
10 m   10 m

'm' is short for metres.

Work out the total lengths of these joined-up pipes.

a

Work out 3 × 10 metres.

b

Work out 5 × 10 metres.

c

d

4 The total length of 15 pipes from question 3 is
15 × 10 m = 150 m
Work out the lengths of these numbers of pipes:

All the digits move to the next highest place.

a 9 pipes **b** 11 pipes **c** 19 pipes **d** 23 pipes
e 7 pipes **f** 35 pipes **g** 42 pipes **h** 44 pipes

5 How many 10 metre pipes would you need to make a pipeline of:
a 40 m **b** 90 m?

6 A bag of cement weighs 10 kg.
a If you need 50 kg of cement, how many bags would you buy?
b If you need 40 kg of cement, how many bags would you buy?
c Lisa can carry 30 kg. How many bags can Lisa carry?
d Look at the picture.
The top bag has split and spilled 3 kg of cement.
What do the four bags weigh now?

You should know how to ...

1 Multiply any whole number by 10 and understand the effect.

▶ 23 × 10 = 230

2 Order a set of positive and negative numbers.

▶

−3 °C is less than 5 °C.

3 Understand the decimal point.

▶

3.6

3 units   6 tenths

4 Use place value to add or subtract mentally.

▶ 25 + 34

Start at 25.

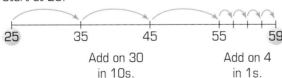

Add on 30 in 10s.   Add on 4 in 1s.

25 + 34 = 59

Check out

1 Write down the answers to

a   7 × 10 =

b   19 × 10 =

c   28 × 10 =

d   143 × 10 =

2 Write these temperatures in order of size, starting with the coldest.

1 °C   2 °C   −3 °C   −4 °C   0 °C   5 °C

The thermometer may help you:

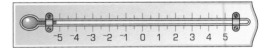

3 In the number 5.4:

a   What does the digit 4 represent?

b   What does the digit 5 represent?

4 Work out these answers in your head. You can use a number line to help.

a   4 + 90 =   b   110 − 50 =

c   52 + 40 =   d   63 − 20 =

e   500 + 700 =   f   1200 − 400 =

g   420 + 76 =   h   580 + 41 =

This unit will show you how to:

▶▶ Use, read and write standard metric units.

▶▶ Suggest suitable units to estimate and measure lengths.

▶▶ Measure and draw lines to the nearest centimetre.

▶▶ Write estimates and readings from scales.

▶▶ Understand that area is measured in squared units.

▶▶ Calculate the perimeter and area of simple shapes.

▶▶ Use the formula in words for the area of a rectangle.

The largest possible area of a football pitch is 11 700 m².

Before you start

You should know how to ...

1 Recognise rectangles.

2 Read scales.

Check in

1 Which of these shapes are rectangles?

a   b   c

d   e   f

2 What reading does each scale show?

a

```
0    5    10
```

b

```
800 ml
700 ml
600 ml
500 ml
400 ml
300 ml
200 ml
100 ml
```

S1.1 Measurements and scales

This spread will show you how to:

▶▶ Use, read and write standard metric units.
▶▶ Suggest suitable units to estimate and measure lengths.
▶▶ Measure and draw lines to the nearest centimetre.
▶▶ Record estimates and readings from scales.

KEYWORDS

Millimetre	Measure
Centimetre	Ruler
Metre	Scale
Kilometre	

There are four common metric units of length.

Millimetres measure very small distances.

Centimetres measure small distances.

Metres measure bigger distances.

Kilometres measure very big distances.

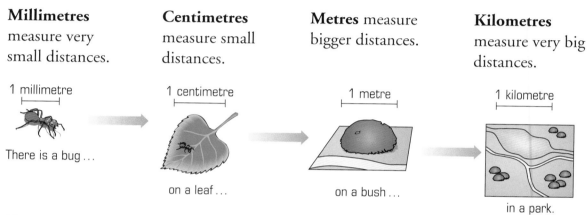

1 millimetre

There is a bug ...

1 centimetre

on a leaf ...

1 metre

on a bush ...

1 kilometre

in a park.

You can measure and draw short lengths using a ruler.

example

a Measure this line in centimetres.

b Draw a line 2 centimetres long.

....

a Make sure you start from the 0 mark.

b Start to draw from 0.

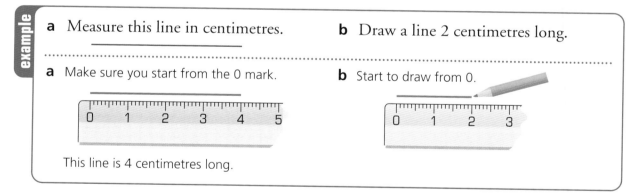

This line is 4 centimetres long.

You should be able to read other scales.

This scale is numbered in 10s.

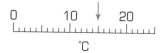

°C

Each small division is 1 °C.
The reading shows 15 °C.

This scale is numbered in 100s.

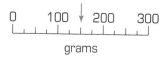

grams

Each small division is 25 grams.
The reading shows 150 grams.

Exercise S1.1

1 Which unit would you use to measure each of these?
Choose your answer from this box:

> millimetre   centimetre   metre   kilometre

a The length of this book.
b The distance from Earth to the Sun.
c The width of your bedroom.
d The length of one of your eyelashes.
e The length of the school playground.
f The length of your arm.
g The distance across your classroom.
h A journey from London to New York.
i The width of a bee's wing.

2 Measure each of these lines in cm.
Make sure you measure from 0.

a
b
c
d
e

3 Draw these lines accurately using a ruler.
  a 3 centimetres   **b** 7 centimetres   **c** 5 centimetres
  d 8 centimetres   **e** 10 centimetres   **f** 1 centimetre

4 What reading does each scale show?

a   20   30   ↓   40

b   120   130   140↓   150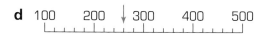

c   0   100   200   ↓   300

d   100   200   ↓   300   400   500

        e **f**   **g**   **h**   **i**   **j**

70   ↓80↓   90 ↓ 100   110 ↓ 120↓ 130 ↓40

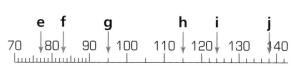

5 **Brain teaser**
This dial cannot be seen properly.
What reading is shown on the dial?

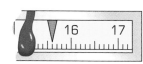

This spread will show you how to:

▶▶ Calculate the perimeter of simple shapes.

KEYWORDS
Centimetres (cm)
Perimeter   Edge
Rectangle   Distance
Shape

Joe is marking the edge of the football pitch.

The distance around the edge is the perimeter.

▶ **The perimeter of a shape is the distance around the edge.**

You can measure perimeter using metric lengths.

'cm' means centimetres.

example

Find the perimeter of this rectangle.

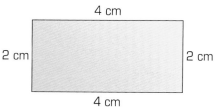

To find the perimeter, add the lengths of the edges together.

2 cm + 4 cm + 2 cm + 4 cm
Perimeter = 12 cm

You need to know the lengths of all the edges.

example

a Work out the missing measurement for this L shape.

b Find the perimeter of the shape.

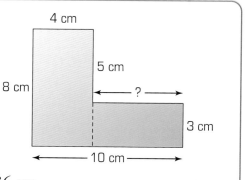

a The base is 10 cm.
The top is 4 cm.
The missing measurement must be 6 cm.

b To find the perimeter you add all six sides:
3 cm + 10 cm + 8 cm + 4 cm + 5 cm + 6 cm = 36 cm

Exercise S1.2

1 These letters are drawn on centimetre squared paper.
The perimeter of the letter **I** is 12 cm.
Find the perimeter of the other letters.

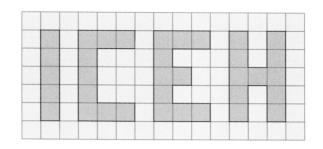

2 Find the perimeter of each shape.

a

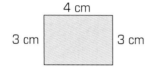

4 cm
3 cm   3 cm

b

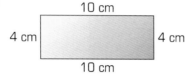

10 cm
4 cm   4 cm
10 cm

c

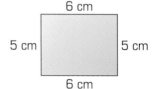

6 cm
5 cm   5 cm
6 cm

d

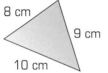

8 cm
9 cm
10 cm

e

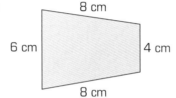

8 cm
6 cm   4 cm
8 cm

f

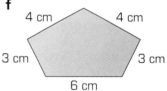

4 cm   4 cm
3 cm   3 cm
6 cm

3 Work out the missing measurement in each shape then find the perimeter.

a

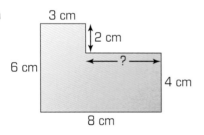

3 cm
2 cm
6 cm   ?
4 cm
8 cm

b

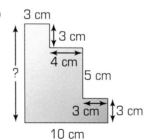

3 cm
3 cm
4 cm
?   5 cm
3 cm   3 cm
10 cm

c

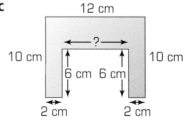

12 cm
?
10 cm   10 cm
6 cm   6 cm
2 cm   2 cm

4 Brain teaser
Use the clues in this drawing to work out the length of the side marked *x*.

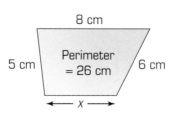

8 cm
5 cm   Perimeter = 26 cm   6 cm
x

S1.3 Area

This spread will show you how to:

▶ Understand that area is measured in squared units.
▶▶ Use the formula in words for the area of a rectangle.

KEYWORDS

Surface   Width
Area   Length
Square   Multiply
Rectangle
Centimetre squares (cm²)

Joe is cutting the grass on the football pitch.

The surface of the pitch is its area.

Area is measured in squares:

This rectangle covers 12 squares.   This rectangle covers 10 squares.

The area is 12 squares.   The area is 10 squares.

> ▶ The surface of a shape is called the area.

This shape is drawn on centimetre squared paper:

The area is 15 centimetre squares.
You write 15 cm² for short.

> ▶ cm² means centimetre squares.

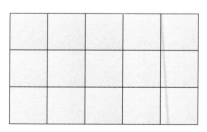

You can use this rule to find the area of the rectangle:

> ▶ Area of rectangle = length × width

The length is 5 cm.
The width is 3 cm.

Area = 5 cm × 3 cm = 15 cm²

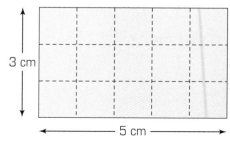

Exercise S1.3

1 These letters are drawn on centimetre squared paper.
The area of the letter H is 11 centimetre squares.
Find the area of the other letters.

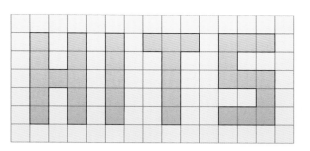

2 How many squares are there in each rectangle?
Write your answer like this:
The area is _____ squares.

a   **b** 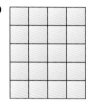 **c** 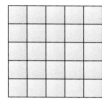 **d**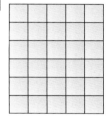

3 To find the area of a rectangle you use this rule:

> Area = length × width

Find the area of these rectangles.
Your answers will be in cm².

a 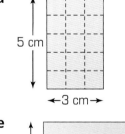 5 cm, 3 cm

b 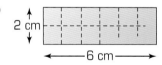 2 cm, 6 cm

c 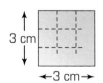 3 cm, 3 cm

d 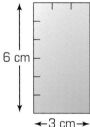 6 cm, 3 cm

e 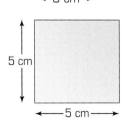 5 cm, 5 cm

f 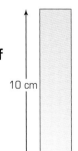 10 cm, 2 cm

g 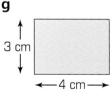 3 cm, 4 cm

h 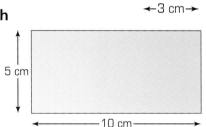 5 cm, 10 cm

4 Brain teaser
The area of this shape is 14 cm².
It is 7 cm wide.
What is the length of the shape?

?   Area = 14 cm²

7 cm

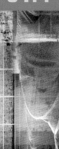

This spread will show you how to:

▶▶ Calculate the perimeter and area of simple shapes.

▶▶ Use the formula in words for the area of a rectangle.

KEYWORDS

Perimeter	Area
Edge	Surface
Length	Rectangle

▶ **The perimeter of a shape is the distance around the edge.**

To find the perimeter of this rectangle ...   ... you add all the edges.

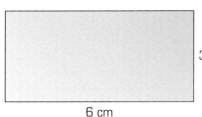

Perimeter = 3 cm + 6 cm + 3 cm + 6 cm
= 18 cm

▶ **The area of a shape is the amount of surface it covers.**

The shape has four sides so you add four lengths.

To find the area of the rectangle, you split it into centimetre squares.

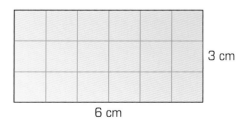

The area is 18 cm^2.

You can use the rule:

▶ **Area of a rectangle = length × width**

Area = 3 cm × 6 cm = 18 cm^2

Exercise S1.4

1 The letter T is drawn on centimetre squared paper.
   a What is the perimeter of the T shape?
   b What is the area of the T shape?

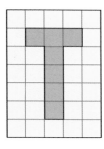

2 These shapes are drawn on centimetre squared paper.
   Find the perimeter and area of each shape.

   a

   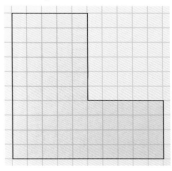

   b

   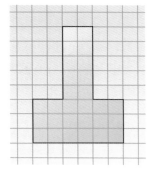

3 Draw these rectangles on squared paper.
   The measurements are the length and the width.
   Find the perimeter and area of each rectangle.
   a 4 cm × 3 cm   b 2 cm × 5 cm   c 4 cm × 6 cm

4 Find the perimeter and area of each garden.
   The measurements are in metres so the area will be in m².

   'm' is short for metre.

   a

   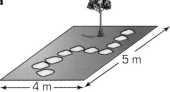

   b

   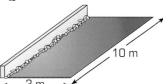

   c

   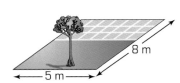

5 **Brain teaser**
   A square has four equal sides.
   The perimeter of the square is 36 cm.
   a What is the length of one side?
   b What is the area of the square?

   Perimeter
   = 36 cm

You should know how to ...

1 Suggest suitable units to estimate and measure lengths.

You use:
- ▶ millimetres to measure very short lengths.
- ▶ centimetres to measure short lengths.
- ▶ metres to measure longer lengths.
- ▶ kilometres to measure very long lengths.

2 Calculate the perimeter and area of rectangles and other simple shapes by counting.

- ▶ The perimeter is the distance around the edge of a shape.

3 Understand and use the formula in words for the area of a rectangle.

> Area of rectangle = length × width

Check out

1 Use some of the units in the box to:
- **a** Estimate the height of your desk.
- **b** Estimate the length of your pencil.

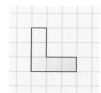

cm   mm   km   m

2 Find the perimeter of this shape:

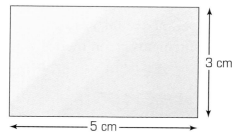

Give your answer in squares.

3 Find the area of this rectangle:

3 cm

5 cm

This unit will show you how to:

▶▶ Read and write fractions.

▶▶ Order simple fractions.

▶▶ Recognise mixed numbers.

▶▶ Use symbols correctly.

▶▶ Begin to write fractions as a division and find simple fractions of numbers and quantities.

▶▶ Divide by 10.

▶▶ Read and write tenths as decimals.

▶▶ Write fractions as a decimal.

▶▶ Record estimates from scales.

▶▶ Begin to understand percentage as the number of parts in every 100.

▶▶ Write tenths as percentages.

▶▶ Find simple percentages of whole numbers.

▶▶ Use all four operations to solve simple word problems.

Each piece of cake is $\frac{1}{7}$ of the whole.

Before you start

You should know how to ...

1 Recognise and find $\frac{1}{2}$ and $\frac{1}{4}$.

2 Find unit fractions of shapes.

Check in

1 Here are 12 cubes:

a How may cubes are in $\frac{1}{2}$ of all the cubes?

b How may cubes are in $\frac{1}{4}$ of all the cubes?

2 Copy this rectangle three times:

On a new copy each time:

a Shade $\frac{1}{2}$ of the rectangle.

b Shade $\frac{1}{3}$ of the rectangle.

c Shade $\frac{1}{4}$ of the rectangle.

Understanding fractions

This spread will show you how to:

▶▶ Read and write fractions.

KEYWORDS

Numerator	Equal
Fair shares	Divided
Part	Fraction
Denominator	Identical

Tim and Tom are sharing a cake.
It is not cut into fair shares.

When the cake is cut fairly, the slices are an equal size.

The cake is divided into two equal parts.
Each part is a $\frac{1}{2}$ (a half).

> ▶ A fraction has two parts:
>
> $\frac{1}{2}$ ◀— **numerator**: tells you how many parts you have.
>
> ◀— **denominator** tells you how many equal parts there are.

The kite is shaded blue and red.

One of the four parts is red.
You write: $\frac{1}{4}$ is red.

$$\frac{1}{4}$$ ◀—1 part is red
◀—there are 4 equal parts

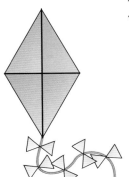

Three of the four parts are blue.
You write: $\frac{3}{4}$ is blue.

$$\frac{3}{4}$$ ◀— 3 parts are blue
◀— there are 4 equal parts

Exercise N2.1

1 Which of these cuts show fair shares?
Answer **X**, **Y** or **Z**.

a X Y Z

b X Y Z

c X Y Z

d X Y Z

2 How many equal parts has each cake been cut into?

a   **b**   **c**   **d**

3 This pentagon is divided into five identical triangles.
Three of the five triangles are blue.
You write: $\frac{3}{5}$ is blue.

For each of these shapes, write a sentence saying what fraction of the shape is blue.

a   **b**   **c**    **d**

4 Write the fraction of each shape in question 3 that is white.

5 This hexagon is made from six identical triangles.
Each triangle is $\frac{1}{6}$ of the hexagon.

$6 \times \frac{1}{6}$ s are one whole.

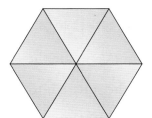

Which of these fractions are equal to one whole?
Answer **Yes** or **No**.

a $\frac{5}{6}$ **b** $\frac{2}{3}$ **c** $\frac{7}{7}$ **d** $\frac{4}{5}$ **e** $\frac{8}{8}$

This spread will show you how to:
- ▶▶ Order simple fractions.
- ▶▶ Recognise mixed numbers.
- ▶▶ Use symbols correctly.

KEYWORDS

Rectangle
Whole   Divide
Part   Square
Fraction
Denominator

These two rectangles are the same size:

$\frac{1}{2}$	$\frac{1}{2}$

This rectangle is divided into $\frac{1}{2}$s.

$\frac{1}{3}$	$\frac{1}{3}$	$\frac{1}{3}$

This rectangle is divided into $\frac{1}{3}$s.

$\frac{1}{2}$ of the rectangle is bigger than $\frac{1}{3}$.

You can write $\frac{1}{2} > \frac{1}{3}$.

These two squares are the same size:

$\frac{1}{3}$	$\frac{1}{3}$	$\frac{1}{3}$

This square is divided into $\frac{1}{3}$s.

$\frac{1}{4}$	$\frac{1}{4}$
$\frac{1}{4}$	$\frac{1}{4}$

This square is divided into $\frac{1}{4}$s.

You cannot compare the red areas easily.

$\frac{1}{3}$ divides the square into 3 parts,

$\frac{1}{4}$ divides the square into 4 parts,

so $\frac{1}{3}$ is larger than $\frac{1}{4}$.

You write: $\frac{1}{3} > \frac{1}{4}$

▶ The **denominator** tells you how many parts the whole is divided into.
It is the bottom part of the fraction.

Exercise N2.2

1 What fraction has each rectangle been divided into?

a   b   c   d   e

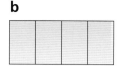  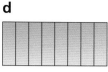 

2 Use your answers to question 1 to compare these fractions.
Use these signs:

> means 'is bigger than'.
< means 'is smaller than'.

a $\frac{1}{4}$ and $\frac{1}{2}$ **b** $\frac{1}{4}$ and $\frac{1}{3}$ **c** $\frac{1}{3}$ and $\frac{1}{8}$ **d** $\frac{1}{2}$ and $\frac{1}{8}$

e $\frac{1}{2}$ and $\frac{1}{3}$ **f** $\frac{1}{3}$ and $\frac{1}{5}$ **g** $\frac{1}{4}$ and $\frac{1}{5}$ **h** $\frac{1}{8}$ and $\frac{1}{5}$

3 Put these fractions into order from the smallest to the largest.
$\frac{1}{8}, \quad \frac{1}{2}, \quad \frac{1}{3}, \quad \frac{1}{5}, \quad \frac{1}{4}$

4 Compare these fractions.
Use the signs > and < to write your answers.
The first question is done for you.

a $\frac{1}{4}$ and $\frac{1}{6}$.

    $\frac{1}{4} > \frac{1}{6}$ (when you divide an amount into 4 parts each
                 part is bigger than when you divide it into 6 parts.)

b $\frac{1}{2}$ and $\frac{1}{3}$ **c** $\frac{1}{8}$ and $\frac{1}{10}$ **d** $\frac{1}{5}$ and $\frac{1}{3}$ **e** $\frac{1}{7}$ and $\frac{1}{2}$

f $\frac{1}{6}$ and $\frac{1}{3}$ **g** $\frac{1}{4}$ and $\frac{1}{9}$ **h** $\frac{1}{20}$ and $\frac{1}{6}$ **i** $\frac{1}{12}$ and $\frac{1}{15}$

5 This square has been divided into four $\frac{1}{4}$s (4 quarters).
The whole shape is $\frac{4}{4}$.

The fraction $\frac{5}{4}$ is greater than one whole because it has 5 quarters.
The fraction $\frac{3}{4}$ is less than one whole because it has 3 quarters.

You write: $\frac{4}{4} = 1; \frac{3}{4} < 1$ and $\frac{5}{4} > 1$

$\frac{1}{4}$	$\frac{1}{4}$
$\frac{1}{4}$	$\frac{1}{4}$

Use these signs to compare these
fractions with one whole unit.

Choose = , > or <

a $\frac{5}{5}$ ☐ 1   **b** $\frac{7}{5}$ ☐ 1   **c** $\frac{2}{5}$ ☐ 1   **d** $\frac{5}{6}$ ☐ 1   **e** $\frac{10}{10}$ ☐ 1   **f** $\frac{3}{2}$ ☐ 1

This spread will show you how to:

▶▶ Find simple fractions of numbers and quantities.
▶▶ Begin to write fractions as a division.

KEYWORDS

Of   Multiply
Divide   Doubling
Half
Times table

Here are 8 buttons.

One half of the buttons are yellow and the other half are grey.

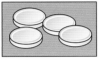

There are 4 yellow buttons and 4 grey buttons.

$\frac{1}{2}$ of 8 is 4.

▶ To find $\frac{1}{2}$ of an amount, you divide the amount by 2.

You can use the 2 times table to help divide larger numbers.

example

Calculate:

a $\frac{1}{2}$ of 18   **b** $\frac{1}{2}$ of 60.

a You know that:
$2 \times \mathbf{9} = 18$
So $18 \div 2 = 9$
So $\frac{1}{2}$ of 18 is 9.

b You know that:
$\frac{1}{2}$ of 6 is 3
So $\frac{1}{2}$ of 60 is 30.

2 ×	2	=	4
2 ×	3	=	6
2 ×	4	=	8
2 ×	5	=	10
2 ×	6	=	12
2 ×	7	=	14
2 ×	8	=	16
2 ×	9	=	18
2 ×	10	=	20

▶ To find $\frac{1}{4}$ of an amount, you divide the amount by 4.

To calculate $\frac{1}{4}$ of 24, you work out $24 \div 4$.

Look for the number that 4 is multiplied by to make 24:

$4 \times 6 = 24$
So $\frac{1}{4}$ of $24 = 6$

4 ×	2	=	8
4 ×	3	=	12
4 ×	4	=	16
4 ×	5	=	20
4 ×	6	=	24
4 ×	7	=	28
4 ×	8	=	32
4 ×	9	=	36
4 ×	10	=	40

Exercise N2.3

1 Half of the buttons in these questions should be coloured yellow.
How many buttons in each group should be yellow?

a  b  c  d

2 Find half of these numbers by dividing by 2.

   a $\frac{1}{2}$ of 6 =   b $\frac{1}{2}$ of 8 =   c $\frac{1}{2}$ of 10 =

   d $\frac{1}{2}$ of 12 =   e $\frac{1}{2}$ of 20 =   f $\frac{1}{2}$ of 40 =

   g $\frac{1}{2}$ of 60 =   h $\frac{1}{2}$ of 80 =   i $\frac{1}{2}$ of 90 =

3 Use counters or drawings to calculate $\frac{1}{4}$ of these amounts.
Write your answers like this: $\frac{1}{4}$ of 4 = 1

a   b   c  d

4 Use the 4 times table to calculate $\frac{1}{4}$ of these amounts.

   a $\frac{1}{4}$ of 20 =   b $\frac{1}{4}$ of 32 =   c $\frac{1}{4}$ of 16 =   d $\frac{1}{4}$ of 24 =

   e $\frac{1}{4}$ of 4 =   f $\frac{1}{4}$ of 40 =   g $\frac{1}{4}$ of 28 =   h $\frac{1}{4}$ of 36 =

5 You can use doubling to extend the 4 times table:

> $\frac{1}{4}$ of 40 = 10 $\frac{1}{4}$ of 32 = 8
> so, $\frac{1}{4}$ of 80 = 20   so, $\frac{1}{4}$ of 64 = 16

Calculate $\frac{1}{4}$ of these amounts.

   a $\frac{1}{4}$ of £28 = £7   b $\frac{1}{4}$ of 36 kg = 9 kg   c $\frac{1}{4}$ of 24 cm = ____

      so, $\frac{1}{4}$ of £56 = ____   so, $\frac{1}{4}$ of 72 kg = ____   so, $\frac{1}{4}$ of 48 cm = ____

6 a When a jar is full it holds 40 sweets.
How many sweets does it hold when it is $\frac{1}{4}$ full?

  b If a jar holds 400 sweets, how many sweets does it hold
when it is only $\frac{1}{4}$ full?

  c If there are 100 sweets in the jar and you eat $\frac{1}{4}$ of them,
how many sweets have you eaten?

This spread will show you how to:

▶▶ Read and write tenths as decimals.
▶▶ Write fractions as a decimal.
▶▶ Record estimates from scales.

KEYWORDS

Tenth	Measure
Decimal	Compare
Equal	Estimate
Scale	Fraction

A decimal scale is divided into ten equal parts.
Each part is one tenth.

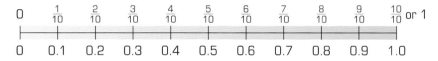

0	$\frac{1}{10}$	$\frac{2}{10}$	$\frac{3}{10}$	$\frac{4}{10}$	$\frac{5}{10}$	$\frac{6}{10}$	$\frac{7}{10}$	$\frac{8}{10}$	$\frac{9}{10}$	$\frac{10}{10}$ or 1
0	0.1	0.2	0.3	0.4	0.5	0.6	0.7	0.8	0.9	1.0

▶ There are two ways to write tenths:
as fractions, $\frac{1}{10}$, $\frac{2}{10}$, ... and as decimals, 0.1, 0.2, ...

You can use a decimal scale to measure parts of a whole.

0.1	0.1	0.1	0.1	0.1	0.1	0.1	0.1	0.1	0.1

There are ten equal parts on this strip. Each part is 0.1 (one tenth) of the strip.

This scale is more than 1 unit long.

The red line is longer than 6 units but less than 7 units.

▶ You use decimals to measure more accurately.

There are 10 spaces between the unit marks.
Each space is one tenth.

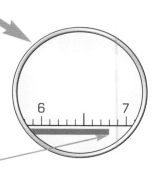

The red line is 8 tenths more than 6 units.
It is 6.8 units long.

Exercise N2.4

1 These strips are one unit long.
What fraction of each strip is red?
Write your answers in two ways: as decimals and as fractions.

a b c d e f g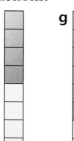

2 Write these fractions as decimals.
a $\frac{4}{10}$ b $\frac{1}{10}$ c $\frac{8}{10}$ d $\frac{2}{10}$ e $\frac{9}{10}$ f $\frac{7}{10}$

3 Draw and shade strips of one unit to show these decimal numbers.
a 0.1   b 0.3   c 0.8   d 0.5   e 0.6   f 0.9

4 Write these decimal numbers in order from the smallest to the largest.
0.9,   0.7,   0.3,   0.5,   0.1,   1.0,   0.6,   0.4

5 Use these signs to compare the fractions and decimals.

> means 'is bigger than'.
< means 'is smaller than'.
= means 'is the same as'.

a $\frac{7}{10}$ and 0.5   b 0.6 and $\frac{6}{10}$ c 0.3 and $\frac{2}{10}$ d $\frac{8}{10}$ and 0.9
e 1.0 and 1   f 0.1 and $\frac{1}{10}$ g 0.7 and $\frac{4}{10}$ h 0.5 and $\frac{1}{2}$

6 Use decimals to estimate the lengths of the red lines.
For example, the first one (a) is about 3.3 units.

a
2   3   4   5

b
4   5   6   7   8   9

c
7   8   9   10   11

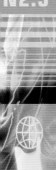

This spread will show you how to:

▶▶ Begin to understand percentage as the number of parts in every 100.

▶▶ Write tenths as percentages.

KEYWORDS

Percent (%) Hundred
Decimal   Fraction
Whole   Equal

Percentages are another way of writing fractions.
Per cent means 'out of one hundred'.

There are ten 10% spaces between 0% and 100%.

0%	10%	20%	30%	40%	50%	60%	70%	80%	90%	100%
0	0.1	0.2	0.3	0.4	0.5	0.6	0.7	0.8	0.9	1.0
0	$\frac{1}{10}$	$\frac{2}{10}$	$\frac{3}{10}$	$\frac{4}{10}$	$\frac{5}{10}$	$\frac{6}{10}$	$\frac{7}{10}$	$\frac{8}{10}$	$\frac{9}{10}$	$\frac{10}{10}$ or 1

Each 10% is the same as $\frac{1}{10}$ or 0.1.

▶ One tenth $= \frac{1}{10} = 0.1 = 10\%$

This cake is divided into ten equal slices.
Each slice of the cake is a tenth of the whole cake

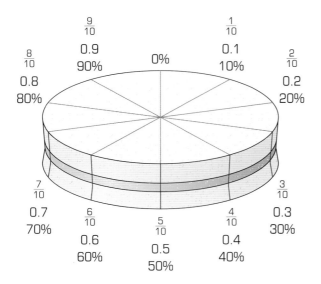

You should know tenths as fractions, decimals and percentages.

Exercise N2.5

1 These cakes are divided into ten equal slices.
What percentage of each cake is red?

a **b** **c** **d** **e**

f **g** **h** **i** **j**

2 Use fractions to say how much of each cake in question 1 is yellow.
The first one has been done for you.
a $\frac{9}{10}$ of the cake is yellow.

3 Shade these percentages on separate drawings of cakes.
a 10% **b** 70% **c** 40% **d** 20% **e** 100%

4 Compare these numbers using the signs:

> > means 'is bigger than'.
> < means 'is smaller than'.
> = means 'is the same as'.

a 40% and $\frac{8}{10}$ **b** $\frac{7}{10}$ and 70% **c** 10% and 0.7 **d** $\frac{9}{10}$ and 80%
e 50% and 0.5 **f** 90% and $\frac{9}{10}$ **g** $\frac{8}{10}$ and 100% **h** 100% and $\frac{10}{10}$

5 The drawing shows a measuring jar.
When it is 90% full, it is 10% empty.
Copy this table and fill in the missing percentages.

Full	90%	80%	30%			15%	100%
Empty	10%			60%	50%		

100%
90%
80%
70%
60%
50%
40%
30%
20%
10%

This spread will show you how to:

▶▶ Find simple percentages of whole numbers.
▶▶ Divide by 10 and understand the effect.

KEYWORDS

Tenth	Hundreds
Divide	Tens
Equal	Units
Group	Digit

Here are 30 beads.

To find $\frac{1}{10}$ of the beads, you divide them into 10 equal groups:

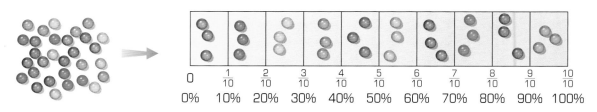

Each group is $\frac{1}{10}$ or 10% of the total.

$\frac{1}{10}$ of 30 = 3   or   10% of 30 = 3

▶ To find $\frac{1}{10}$ or 10% of an amount, you divide the amount by 10.

When you divide by 10 the digits move to the next lowest place:

$30 \div 10 = 3$

The tens digit moves to the units:

tens	**units**
3	0
	3

$170 \div 10 = 17$

The hundred moves to the tens place and the tens move to the units:

hundreds	**tens**	**units**
1	7	0
	1	7

All the digits move to the next lowest place.

▶ To divide an amount by 10, you move the digits to the next lowest place.

Exercise N2.6

1 Divide these amounts by 10.

   a   90 kg ÷ 10 =   **b**   50 cm ÷ 10 =   **c**   £70 ÷ 10 =   **d** £100 ÷ 10 =

   e 150 m ÷ 10 =   **f** 190 mm ÷ 10 =   **g** 320 ℓ ÷ 10 =   **h** 750 g ÷ 10 =

2 To find 10% of an amount, you calculate $\frac{1}{10}$ of the amount.
Calculate 10% of each of these weights.

  a   **b**   **c**   **d**   **e**

3 This is the price tag of a pair of trainers in a sale.
If you buy the trainers in the sale, how much will you save?

4 This counting stick is 50 cm long.

There are 10 coloured sections, so each section is 10%.
10% of 50 cm is 50 cm ÷ 10.
So, 50 cm ÷ 10 = 5 cm.

  a This counting stick is 120 cm long.
      Each section is 10% of the stick.
      How long is each section?

  b If the stick weighs 500 g, what will 10% of the stick weigh?
  c How much will 20% of the stick weigh?

5 This group of students is 10% of the school basketball club.

  a How many students are there in the whole basketball club?
  b Only 20% of the students turned up for training. How many students turned up?

You should know how to ...

1 Divide by 10 and understand the effect.

▶ $130 \div 10 = 13$

hundreds	tens	units
1	3	0
	1	3

2 Read and write tenths as decimals.

▶

3 units   6 tenths

3 Write fractions as a decimal.

▶ $\frac{1}{10} = 0.1$

Check out

1 Work out these divisions in your head:

a $60 \div 10 =$

b $700 \div 10 =$

c $4000 \div 10 =$

2 Write as a decimal number:

a six tenths

b twenty three and seven tenths.

3 **a** Write these decimals as fractions:

0.5   0.75   0.9

b Write these fractions as decimals:

$\frac{3}{10}$ $\frac{7}{10}$ $\frac{1}{4}$

1 Data and probability

This unit will show you how to:

- ▶▶ Solve a problem by representing and interpreting data in tables, charts and diagrams.
- ▶▶ Discuss the chance or likelihood of particular events.

- ▶▶ Find the mode of a set of data.
- ▶▶ Order numbers.
- ▶▶ Begin to find the median of a set of data.
- ▶▶ Begin to find the mean of a set of data.
- ▶▶ Begin to use words to describe probability.

It can be hard to find the 'average' person.

Before you start

You should know how to ...

1 Order numbers.

Check in

1 Write these numbers in order, starting with the smallest.
   a 3   5   2   4   1
   b 7   9   11   8   3
   c 2   7   1   4   5   3
   d 4   2   12   7   8   6

2 Recognise fractions of a whole.

2 What fraction of each circle is red?

   a   b   c

This spread will show you how to:
- ▶▶ Find the mode of a set of data.
- ▶▶ Read and interpret data in tables, graphs and charts.

KEYWORDS

Data	Triangle
Mode	Square
Modal	Circle

Here is a collection of shapes:

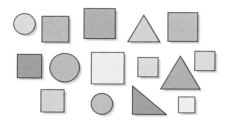

The most common shape is a square.
The square is the mode.

The chart shows a survey of favourite snacks:

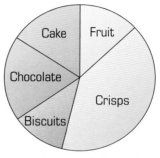

Most people voted for crisps.
Crisps are the mode.

You can say that:

the square is the modal shape   and   crisps are the modal flavour.

▶ The **mode** is the value in the data that occurs most often.

example

The marks out of 10 in a test were:

3   4   8   8   9   6   7   8   5

What is the modal mark?

Write the marks in order:

3   4   5   6   7   8   8   8   9

The modal mark is 8. It occurs most often.

It is easy to read the mode from a diagram.

In this chart, there are more red cars than any other colour.

The modal colour is red.

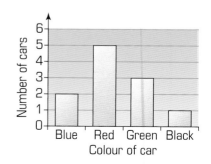

Exercise D1.5

1 There is a ball hidden under one cup in each question.
What are your chances of picking the correct cup?

a

b

c

One chance in ___ or $\frac{1}{?}$.   One chance in ___ or $\frac{1}{?}$.   One chance in ___ or $\frac{1}{?}$.

2 There is one ace in each of these sets of cards.
What are the chances of picking the ace?

a    **b**    **c**

3 What are Jenny's chances of winning in each of these games?
Write your answer as a fraction.

a

There is one ace.

b

One number wins.

c
Lucky Numbers

20	45	16	14
19	9	38	8
12	27	55	12
33	41	7	15

One number wins.

d

Lucky Dip

One package contains
a prize.

4 Find the chance of each arrow stopping on a red section.
Write your answer as a fraction.

a 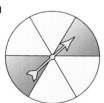   **b** 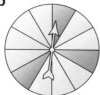   **c**    **d**    **e**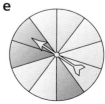

This spread will show you how to:
▶▶ Begin to use words to describe probability.
▶▶ Discuss the probability of particular events.

KEYWORDS
Certain   Impossible
Probability   Likely
Unlikely
Equal chance

When you flip a coin it can land on heads or tails.

It has an equal chance of landing on heads or on tails.

You can place the likelihood of an event on this scale:

Impossible   Unlikely   Equal chance   Likely   Certain

▶ **Probability is a measure of the likelihood of an event.**

An impossible event has no chance of happening at all.
The probability of it happening is 0.

You will definitely not turn green tonight – it is impossible!

A certain event will definitely happen.
The probability of it happening is 1.

You will definitely be older tomorrow – it is certain!

▶ **All probability can be measured on a scale of 0 to 1.**

0                    $\frac{1}{2}$ 1

Impossible
You will eat
a blue apple.

Equal chance or $\frac{1}{2}$
The next person to
be born in the UK
will be a girl.

Certain
The sun will
rise tomorrow.

Exercise D1.6

1 There are 10 beads in a bag.
  a There are three green beads.
    What is the chance of picking a green bead?
  b There are seven yellow beads.
    What is the chance of picking a yellow bead?
  c There are no blue beads.
    What is the chance of picking a blue bead?

2 To win, the arrow must 'land' on blue.
Each probability scale shows the likelihood of winning
with a certain spinner.
Match each spinner with one of the probability scales.

a   **b**   **c**

d   **e**   **f**

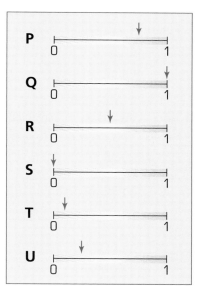

3 A certain event has a probability of 1.
An impossible event has a probability of 0.
For each event copy the scale, and draw and label an
arrow to show its probability

  a By flapping your arms you will fly.

  b Jamie is holding a brick.
    When he lets it go it will drop to the floor.

  c When you flip a coin it will land on heads.

You should know how to …

1 Find the mode of a set of data.

▸ The mode is the value that occurs most often.

2 Discuss the chance or likelihood of particular events.

Check out

1 Here are the shoe sizes of some students in 7W:

5   6   3   3   3   4   2   5

What is the mode?

2 Match one of these words to each of the statements:

CERTAIN   LIKELY   POSSIBLE   IMPOSSIBLE

a   I will eat food next month.
b   It will snow next Christmas.
c   I will see a live dinosaur on my way home.
d   My best friend will grow taller than me.
e   I will drink carrot juice later.

This unit will show you how to:

▶▶ Write expressions using letters.

▶▶ Know how to add and subtract using symbols.

▶▶ Solve problems by adding and subtracting.

If there are 10 doughnuts in a C box but 6 in a B box, which should I buy?

You can use symbols to help you work out problems.

Before you start

You should know how to ...

1 Understand that subtraction is the inverse of addition.

2 Find the perimeter of a shape.
  ▶ The perimeter of a shape is the distance around the edge.

Check in

1 Copy and complete these subtraction and addition sums.

  a $13 - 7 = 6$ so $7 + \underline{\quad} = 13$

  b $20 - 8 = 12$ so $\underline{\quad} + 8 = 20$

  c $18 - 12 = 6$ so $\underline{\quad} + 6 = 18$

2 Find the perimeter of each shape.

  a
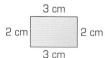

  b

This spread will show you how to:
▶▶ Write expressions using letters.

KEYWORDS
Symbol   Unknown
Represent

This bag holds some marbles.
You do not know exactly how many.

You can use a letter to stand for the number of marbles.

n
marbles

Joel has a bag of *n* marbles.
He gives two marbles to Anita.

I started with *n* marbles then I gave away two marbles, so I have *n* − 2 marbles left.

These people all start with bags of *n* marbles.

Sonia adds five marbles to her bag.

I now have *n* + 5 marbles.

George has three identical bags of marbles.

I now have 3 × *n* marbles.

Marcus shares his marbles equally with Ali.

I now have $\frac{n}{2}$ marbles.

▶ You can use a letter to stand for an unknown number.

You can use any letter.

Exercise A2.1

1 This machine sells sweets.
When it is full there are *n* sweets inside.
Use the symbol *n* to represent the number of sweets in these questions.
The machine starts off full for each question.

  a Jim buys 10 sweets. How many sweets are left in the machine?

  b Sue buys 4 sweets. How many sweets are left?

  c Dinesh buys 20 sweets. How many sweets are left?

  d Tim buys half of the sweets. How many sweets are left?

  e Leroy has lost his money and cannot buy any sweets. How many sweets are left in the machine?

2 There are *b* sweets inside this jar.
There are some sweets on the table.
How many sweets are there altogether?

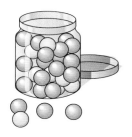

3 There are *c* flowers in a field.

  a How many flowers are there in two identical fields?

  b Four people pick all the flowers in a field.
    They each pick the same amount.
    How many flowers does each person pick?

  c 50 new flowers grow overnight in a field.
    How many flowers are there now altogether?

4 Use your own symbols to describe the total numbers of items in these pictures.

  a

 and another

  b

 and another

This spread will show you how to:
▶▶ Write expressions using letters.

KEYWORDS
Symbol	Subtraction
Addition	Like
Group	

This game is all about **addition**.

You add two blocks to give the block directly below.

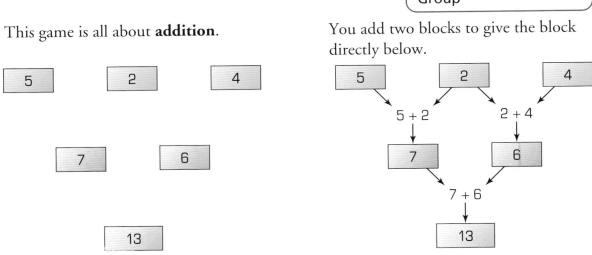

You can play the same game using symbols.
The symbols stand for numbers so you can add them like ordinary numbers.

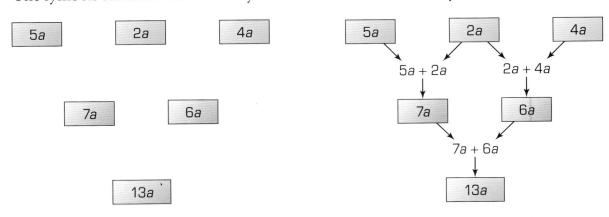

$5a$, $2a$ and $4a$ are called like symbols because they are all alike.
They are all as.

You can group like symbols together by addition:
$2a + 4a = 6a$
The as are grouped together to make $6a$.

Exercise A2.5

In this exercise, the symbols stand for the number of doughnuts in each size of box.

$s = 3$ $m = 6$ $l = 10$

1 How many doughnuts are there in:
  a 2 small boxes?
  b 3 medium boxes?
  c 5 large boxes?

2 How many small boxes do you need to pack 6 doughnuts?

3 How many doughnuts are there in:
  a 1 medium box and 2 doughnuts
  b 2 small boxes and 1 doughnut?

4 Write the number of doughnuts in these situations:
The first one is done for you.
  a $s + 4$
    $s + 4$ means $3 + 4 = 7$ doughnuts.
  b $s + 3 =$ **c** $m + 5 =$ **d** $s + 8 =$ **e** $l + 5 =$
  f $m + 6 =$ **g** $l + 9 =$ **h** $s - 1 =$ **i** $l + 9 =$

5 In 2 large boxes there are 2×10 doughnuts $= 20$ doughnuts.
You write $2 \times l = 20$
Work out how many doughnuts are there in these amounts.
  a 3 small boxes   **b** 5 small boxes   **c** 2 medium boxes
  d 4 large boxes   **e** $10 \times m$ **f** $20 \times s$
  g $10 \times l$ **h** $6 \times m$

6 Is $10 \times s$ doughnuts the same number as $3 \times l$ doughnuts?

You should know how to ...

1 Write an expression in words.

▶ $n + 2$ means 2 more than n.

▶ $n - 3$ means 3 less than n.

▶ $4n$ means 4 times n.

2 Write an expression using letters.

Check out

1 Write each of these statements in words:

a $n + 3$

b $n - 4$

c $2n$

2 a There are n cars in a car park.
3 more cars are parked.
How many cars are parked altogether?
Write: n __ __ cars.

b There are n pears in a bag.
Jules eats 2 pears.
How many pears are left?
Write: n __ __ pears.

This unit will show you how to:

▶▶ Use units of time.

▶▶ Use 24-hour clock notation.

▶▶ Read and plot coordinates in the first quadrant.

The hands of a clock make an angle.

Before you start

You should know how to ...

1 Read the time on an analogue clock.

2 Visualise 2-D shapes.

3 Extend number sequences.

Check in

1 What time does each clock show?

a  b

2 Name these shapes:

a   b

3 Find the next number in each sequence:

a 1, 3, 5, 7, ___

b 2, 5, 8, 11, ___

c 18, 14, 10, 6, ___

This spread will show you how to:
▶▶ Use units of time.
▶▶ Use 24-hour clock notation.

KEYWORDS
Analogue   Clock
Digital   am
Time   pm

You should know these units of time:

getting larger		
Second	There are 60 seconds in a minute.
Minute	There are 60 minutes in an hour.
Hour	There are 24 hours in a day.
Day	There are 7 days in a week.
Week	There are 52 weeks in a year.
Month	There are 12 months in a year.
Year	There are 365 days in a year (and 366 in a leap year).

You read the time on a clock or a calendar.

An analogue clock is numbered from 1 to 12.
You use **am** for times before midday.

The clock shows 8.30 am.

You use **pm** for times after midday.

The clock shows 8.30 pm.

A digital clock uses the 24-hour clock.

This scale will help you convert between analogue and digital times.

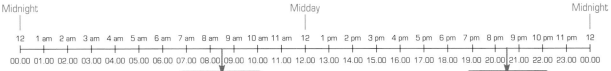

Midnight		Midday		Midnight

12 1 am 2 am 3 am 4 am 5 am 6 am 7 am 8 am 9 am 10 am 11 am 12 1 pm 2 pm 3 pm 4 pm 5 pm 6 pm 7 pm 8 pm 9 pm 10 pm 11 pm 12

00.00 01.00 02.00 03.00 04.00 05.00 06.00 07.00 08.00 09.00 10.00 11.00 12.00 13.00 14.00 15.00 16.00 17.00 18.00 19.00 20.00 21.00 22.00 23.00 00.00

This clock shows 8.30 am.

This clock shows 8.30 pm.

Exercise S2.1

1 Choose the unit of time you would use to measure these events.

> seconds   minutes   hours   days   weeks   months   years

  a Tying your shoe lace.
  b You are asked how old you are.
  c The amount you sleep each night.
  d The length of your summer holidays.
  e The time it takes to run 100 metres.
  f The time it takes to boil an egg.

2 Here are the timings of Kim's day.

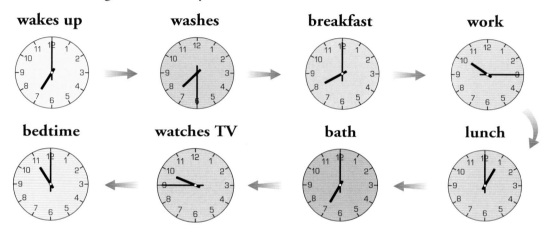

  a What is Kim doing at 7 pm?
  b Does Kim have lunch at 1 am or 1 pm?
  c What is she doing at eight o'clock?
  d Where is Kim at a quarter past ten am?
  e What is Kim doing at 7.30 am?
  f What is Kim doing at a quarter to ten pm?
  g What time does Kim go to bed?

3 Match the times on the analogue clocks with the same time on a digital clock.

4 Challenge
Work out your age in hours to the nearest hour.
Use a calculator to help you.

This spread will show you how to:

▶▶ Read and plot coordinates in the first quadrant.

You can describe the position of a point on this grid.

To find the letter A, you count:

3 across   then   2 up.

The letter A is at the point (3, 2).

(3, 2) is a pair of values called coordinates.

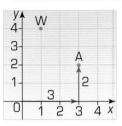

▶ Coordinates fix the position of a point on a grid.

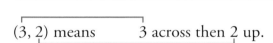

(3, 2) means   3 across then 2 up.

You write coordinate pairs in brackets, separated by a comma:

(1, 4) means   1 across then 4 up.

The letter W is at (1, 4).

▶ In a coordinate pair, you count across first then up.

---

example

Plot the points K = (2, 3) and M = (3, 1) on a coordinate grid.

Number the lines, not the squares.

K is at (2, 3).

Count 2 across and 3 up (follow the red arrows).

M is at (3, 1).

Count 3 across and 1 up (follow the blue arrows).

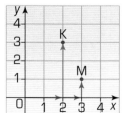

You walk across the hall then up the stairs.

Exercise S2.2

1 The map shows positions of some places.

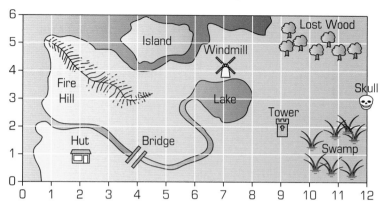

What will you find at these coordinates?
a (2, 1)   **b** (7, 4)   **c** (9, 2)   **d** (4, 1)   **e** (12, 3)

2 Use the map in question 1.
Where would you be standing if you were at these coordinates?
a (11, 1)   **b** (2, 4)   **c** (10, 5)   **d** (7, 3)   **e** (5, 5)

3 The coordinate grid shows the positions of some letters.

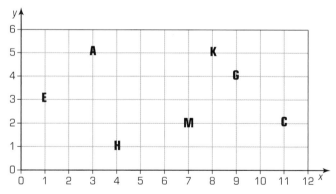

a Write down the coordinates of the letter **A**.
b Write down the coordinates of the letter **C**.
c Write down the coordinates of the letter **E**.
d Write down the coordinates of the letter **G**.
e Write down the coordinates of the letter **M**.
f Write down the coordinates of the letters **H** and **K**.

4 Challenge
What are the coordinates of the point midway between letters
H and **K** in question 3?

S2.3 Coordinates and shapes

This spread will show you how to:

▶▶ Read and plot coordinates in the first quadrant.

KEYWORDS
Coordinates Grid
Triangle   Rectangle
Point   Pattern

A triangle has three sides.

You can join points A, B and C
to make a triangle:

A has coordinates (4, 5)
B has coordinates (6, 1)
C has coordinates (1, 2).

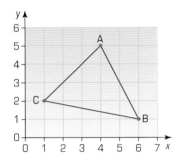

example

Plot these points and join them in turn to
make a shape:

(2, 4)   (6, 4)   (6, 1)   (2, 1)   (2, 4)

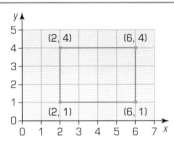

The shape is a rectangle.

Patterns in coordinates

The coordinates of points on a line make a
pattern:

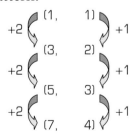

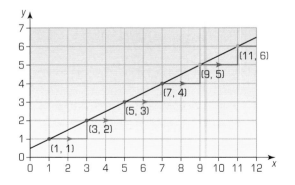

You can find the next points by continuing
the pattern:

Exercise S2.3

1 a Write the coordinates of the points R, S and T.

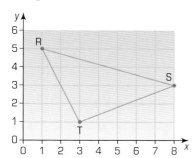

b Write the coordinates of the points J, K, L and M.

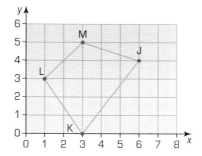

2 Write the coordinates of the points A, B, C, D, E and F.

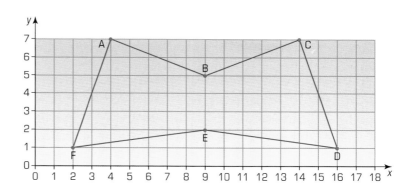

3 Draw four coordinate grids.
Number the axes from 0 to 8.
Plot each set of coordinates on a separate grid.
Join the coordinates to make a shape.

a (1, 1)   (3, 6)   (7, 2)   (1, 1)

b (1, 6)   (6, 6)   (4, 1)   (2, 1)   (1, 6)

c (5, 1)   (4, 4)   (1, 5)   (4, 8)   (8, 4)   (5, 1)

d (1, 5)   (3, 5)   (4, 7)   (5, 5)   (7, 5)   (4, 1)   (1, 5)

You can copy this grid

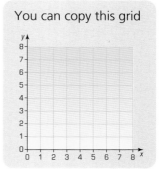

4 The first three coordinates marked on this line are:
(5, 3)   (6, 4)   (7, 5)
What would the next three coordinates be?

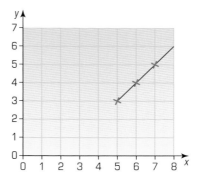

You should know how to ...

1 Use 24-hour clock notation.

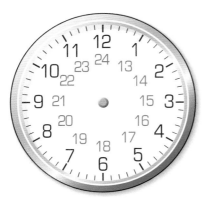

2 Read and plot coordinates in the first quadrant.

Check out

1 Copy and complete this table:

24-hour	12-hour
20:00	8 pm
10:45	
	6.15 pm
	2 am
	9.20 pm
11:30	

2 Write down the coordinates of each of the points marked with a letter.

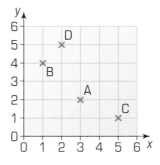

This unit will show you how to:

⏩ Solve a problem by organising, representing and interpreting data in tables, charts and diagrams including:
- ▶ Venn and Carroll diagrams
- ▶ frequency tables
- ▶ pictograms
- ▶ bar charts.

What birds can you see from your window in one morning?
- ☐ Starling
- ☐ Robin
- ☐ Bluetit
- ☐ House Sparrow

You can show lots of different information on a chart.

Before you start

You should know how to ...

1 Use tally marks.
- ▶ 卌 I means 6.

2 Interpret data in simple tables.

Check in

1 What number is represented by each of these tallies?
- **a** |||
- **b** 卌 |||
- **c** 卌 卌 |||

2 The table shows the way students travel to school.

Transport	Bus	Car	Bike	Train	Walk
Frequency	8	11	6	5	6

How many students come by train?

This spread will show you how to:

▶▶ Organise data into Venn and Carroll diagrams.

KEYWORDS

Sort	Overlap
Circle	Triangle
Quadrilateral	
Carroll diagram	
Venn diagram	

Cassie is sorting these shapes:

She sorts them by colour:

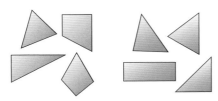

then sorts them by the number of sides:

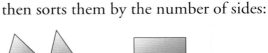

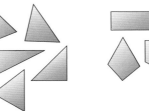

She can use a Carroll diagram to sort all the red triangles:

	Triangle	Not triangle
Red		
Not red		

She can also organise them in a Venn diagram.

example

Draw a Venn diagram to show Cassie's shapes.

You put all the red triangles in the overlap.

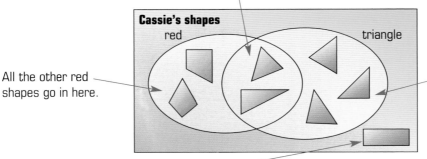

All the other red shapes go in here.

All the other triangles go in here.

Any other shapes go outside the circles.

Exercise D2.1

1 Some of these marbles are red and some are yellow.

How many marbles are red and how many are not red?

Copy and complete this diagram to show the answer.

Red	Not red

2 Some of the marbles in question 1 are small and others are not.

How many marbles are yellow and small?

Copy and complete this Carroll diagram to show the answer.

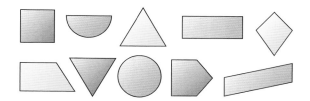

	Small	Not small
Yellow		
Not yellow		

3 Draw a large Carroll diagram like this:

	Quadrilateral	Not quadrilateral
Blue		
Not blue		

Remember:
A quadrilateral has four sides.

It should almost fill your page.
Sketch and label each of these shapes into your diagram.

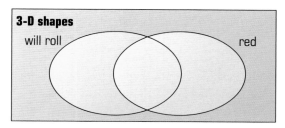

4 Copy this Venn diagram.

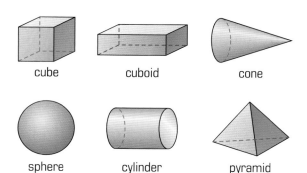

cube   cuboid   cone

sphere   cylinder   pyramid

Write the names of these 3-D shapes in the correct places.

5 Decide on a different way to sort the shapes in question 4.
Draw a Carroll diagram. Add labels and complete your diagram.

This spread will show you how to:

▶▶ Interpret Venn and Carroll diagrams.
▶▶ Interpret data in tables.

KEYWORDS

Sort   Multiple
Table   Carroll diagram
Venn diagram

Ravi sorted some vehicles into this Carroll diagram:

	Car	Not car
Driven by men	3	4
Not driven by men	7	5

3 cars were driven by men.
5 other vehicles were not driven by men.

There were 3 + 7 = 10 cars altogether.

This Venn diagram shows multiples of 3 and multiples of 4:

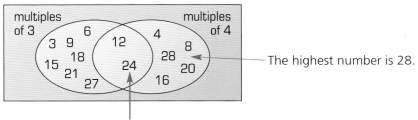

The highest number is 28.

12 and 24 are multiples of 3 **and** multiples of 4.

You can read information from frequency tables.

example

The table shows the favourite colours of class 7A.

a How many different colours were there?
b Which colour got three votes?
c What was the most popular colour?
d How many more students preferred blue than red?

Colour	Votes
Red	5
Green	10
Blue	8
Orange	2
Purple	3

a There were five colours:
   red, green, blue, orange and purple.
b Purple got three votes.
c Green – it got the most votes with 10.
d Red got five votes and blue got eight votes.
   8 – 5 = 3
   Three more students preferred blue than red.

Exercise D2.2

1 This Carroll diagram shows some trees from a park.

	Evergreen	Not evergreen
Trees with berries	holly yew	rowan elder hawthorn
Trees with no berries	fir pine cedar	oak beech

Which trees:

a are evergreen

b have no berries

c are not evergreen

d are not evergreen and have berries

e have berries and are evergreen?

2 One of the numbers in this Venn diagram is in the wrong place.

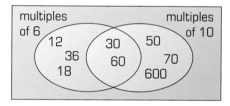

Which number is in the wrong place?
Where should it be?

3 A hotel manager carried out a survey to find the most popular breakfast foods.

a Which was the most popular?

b Which was more popular, cereal or fruit?

c How many more people chose bacon and egg than yoghurt?

d Which food might the manager not serve again? Why?

Breakfast foods

Cereal	27
Fruit	19
Bacon and egg	26
Yoghurt	8
Toast	69
Kippers	1

4 Challenge
How many people took part in the survey in question 3?

This spread will show you how to:

▶▶ Organise data in simple frequency tables.

KEYWORDS

Table   Frequency

Tally   Count

Pritesh and Maria run the school tuck shop.

They want to know how much fruit to buy so none is wasted.

They ask their class which fruit they prefer.
They make a list:

Banana	Banana	Banana	Apple	Banana	Orange
Orange	Banana	Orange	Pear	Banana	Orange
Orange	Apple	Orange	Banana	Pear	Banana
Orange	Grapes	Orange	Pear	Banana	
Pear	Apple	Pear	Banana	Grapes	

They put the results in a table:

They tally the data in 5s so it is easier to count.
卌 means 5 people.

Fruit	Tally	Frequency
Apple	III	
Banana	卌 卌	
Grapes	II	
Orange	卌 III	
Pear	卌	

They count up the tallies to find the total votes for each fruit.

This is the frequency.

Fruit	Tally	Frequency
Apple	III	3
Banana	卌 卌	10
Grapes	II	2
Orange	卌 III	8
Pear	卌	5

▶ You can collect data using a tally.
You count the tallies to find the frequencies.

Exercise D2.3

1 In a survey of water sports,

126 people chose water-skiing,   239 chose sailing,
142 chose surfing and   625 chose swimming.

Copy and complete the frequency table to show this information:

Watersport	Water-skiing	Sailing	Surfing	Swimming
Frequency	126			

2 Millie asked her friends which soap operas they watch.
The answers were:

Coronation St	Neighbours	Coronation St	Neighbours	EastEnders
Emmerdale	Coronation St	Neighbours	Emmerdale	Coronation St
EastEnders	Neighbours	Emmerdale	EastEnders	Emmerdale
EastEnders	EastEnders	EastEnders	Coronation St	EastEnders
Coronation St	Coronation St	Neighbours	EastEnders	Neighbours

Copy and complete this tally chart to show the results.

Count up the tallies and complete the frequency column.

Soap opera	Tally	Frequency
Coronation Street		
Neighbours		
Emmerdale		
EastEnders		

3 Ruby asked her classmates how many brothers and sisters they have.
Here are the answers:

1	0	3	1	1	1	2	2	0	4
1	2	1	0	1	2	2	3	1	1
0	4	1	1	2	1	3	1	2	

Copy and complete this frequency table to show the results.

Number of brothers and sisters	Tally	Frequency
0		
1		
2		
3		
4		

4 Pierre asked his classmates how many pets they have.
Organise his results in a frequency table:

3	0	1	2	1	0	2	1	1
1	2	1	3	0	5	1	2	1
1	2	0	2	2	1	1	1	

This spread will show you how to:

▶▶ Organise data into pictograms.

KEYWORDS
Display   Key
Data   Survey
Pictogram   Represent

Maria and Pritesh want to display the results of their survey.

They use a pictogram showing a banana for each vote.

Favourite fruits

Apple	🍌🍌🍌
Banana	🍌🍌🍌🍌🍌🍌🍌🍌
Grapes	🍌🍌
Orange	🍌🍌🍌🍌🍌🍌🍌🍌
Pear	🍌🍌🍌🍌🍌
	Number of people

Three people voted for Apple.

The most popular fruit was Banana

▶ **A pictogram uses pictures to stand for items.**

Maria collects more data by asking another class.

Fruit	Tally	Frequency
Apple	卌 II	7
Banana	卌 卌 卌	15
Grapes	卌 I	6
Orange	卌 卌 II	12
Pear	IIII	4

There are lots of results so she uses a key:

1 orange   🟠   represents 2 people.
So half an orange ◖   represents 1 person.

The pictogram looks like this:

Favourite fruit

	Number of people
Apple	🟠🟠🟠◖
Banana	🟠🟠🟠🟠🟠🟠🟠◖ ←
Grapes	🟠🟠🟠
Orange	🟠🟠🟠🟠🟠🟠
Pear	🟠🟠

15 people voted for banana.

Make the key clear so everyone can understand the chart.

Key: 🟠 represents 2 people

Exercise D2.4

1 Liam invites 8 boys and 6 girls to his party.
Copy and complete the pictogram to show who he has invited to his party.

People at a party

Girls	🙂 🙂
Boys	
Number of people	

🙂 = 1 person

2 The frequency table shows what sort of Christmas tree the students in class 7C have.

Copy and complete the pictogram to represent this data.

Type of Christmas tree	Frequency
Real tree	9
Fake tree	11
No tree	4

Type of Christmas tree

Real tree	
Fake tree	
No tree	
Number of people	

△ = 1 person

3 The table shows the average hours of sunshine each day in Goldtown.

Copy and complete the pictogram to display this data.

Month	Hours of sunshine
January	2
February	4
March	4
April	6
May	8
June	11

Amount of sunshine

January	
February	
March	
April	
May	
June	
Number of hours	

☼ = 2 hours

4 The table shows the holiday destinations of some people in August one year.

Draw a pictogram to represent this data.
Use a key of one item to represent five people.

Holiday destination	Frequency
Edinburgh	15
London	20
Malaga	30
Paris	15
Orlando	25

This spread will show you how to:

▶▶ Interpret pictograms and bar charts.

KEYWORDS

Survey   Bar chart
Pictogram   Scale
Represent   Key

The pictogram shows students' favourite cold drinks.

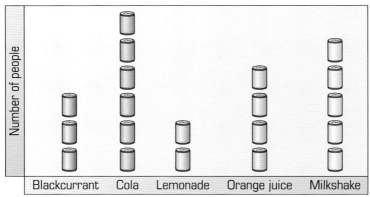

Favourite drink

Key:  = 5 people

4 × 5 = 20 people
voted for orange juice.

▶ A pictogram uses pictures to display data.
You use a key to show what each picture represents.

The bar chart shows favourite types of chocolate bars.

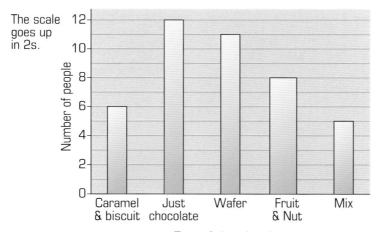

The scale goes up in 2s.

Type of chocolate bar

11 people voted for wafers.

▶ A bar chart uses bars to display data.
You use a scale to show what each bar represents.

Exercise D2.5

1 The bar chart shows the results of a
traffic survey.

  a How many more cars than buses and
lorries are there?

  b How much of the traffic was not cars?

  c How many cars and lorries do you
estimate will go past in two minutes?

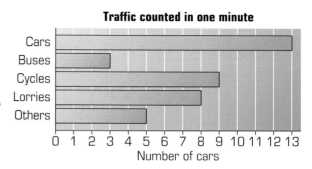

Traffic counted in one minute

2 The Blackpool Tourist Board surveyed
270 people on how they travelled.
The results are shown in the pictogram:

  a How many people voted for taxi?

  b How many people voted for bicycle?

  c How many people in total voted for
taxi or tramcar?

  d How many more people preferred to
use a car than a bus?

Travelling around Blackpool

☺ represents 10 people

3 The bar charts show how students travel to school on
wet days and on dry days.

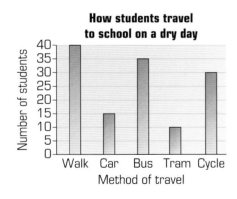

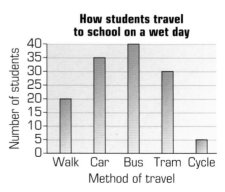

  a How many students travel by bus on a wet day?

  b How many students cycle on a dry day?

  c How many more students walk to school on a dry day than on a wet day?

  d How many fewer students cycle on a wet day than on a dry day?

4 Challenge

How many students took part in the survey in question 3?

You should know how to ...

1 Interpret data in tables, charts and diagrams.

2 Represent data on a bar chart.

Check out

1 The bar chart shows the number of people using the library at certain times:

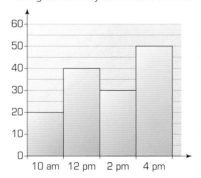

a How many people were in the library at 12 pm?

b At what time was the library quietest?

c What was the most popular time to use the library? Why?

2 The table shows the number of goals scored by City last season.

Number of goals	Frequency
0	2
1	2
2	6
3	5
4	4
5	1

Copy and complete the bar chart to show the information.

Exercise N3.2

1 Work out each of these amounts.
   a Double £5   **b** Double £3   **c** Double £10
   d Double 8 cm   **e** Double £20   **f** Double 50 m

2 Measure the sides of this triangle.
   Double the measurements and write them down.
   Side a =   cm, double side a =   cm.
   Side b =   cm, double side b =   cm.
   Side c =   cm, double side c =   cm.

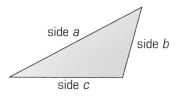

3 Here are the first 10 numbers in the 3 times table.

3 times table	3	6	9	12	15	18	21	24	27	30
6 times table	6		18			36			54	

   a Copy the table.
   b Double each number to make the 6 times table.
      Four numbers have been doubled for you.

4 Here are the first 10 numbers in the 5 times table.

5 times table	5	10	15	20	25	30	35	40	45	50
10 times table	10								90	

   a Copy the table.
   b Use doubling to write the 10 times table in the second row.

5 Use doubling to answer these questions.
   a 22×4 **b** 12×4 **c** 32×4
   d 15×4 **e** 14×4 **f** 16×4

> Jot down your
> working to help you:
> 22×4
> $22 \times 2 = 44$
> $44 \times 2 = 88$
> or even just
> $44 \quad 88$

6 To multiply a number by 6, you double it then multiply by 3.
   Use this method to work out:
   a 15×6 **b** 14×6 **c** 20×6
   d 30×6 **e** 31×6 **f** 21×6

7 To multiply a number by 8, you double it three times.
   Use doubling to work out:
   a 13×8 **b** 15×8 **c** 16×8
   d 20×8 **e** 21×8 **f** 31×8

N3.3 Multiplying decimals by 10

This spread will show you how to:

▶▶ Use tenths written as a decimal and know what each digit represents.

▶▶ Multiply decimals by 10.

KEYWORDS

Decimal   Tens
Place value   Units
Hundreds   Tenths
Decimal point

This line is between 3 cm and 4 cm long.

It is **3.5 cm long.**

3 whole centimetres   5 tenths of a centimetre

▶ The decimal point separates the units from the tenths.

The digits of decimals numbers have their own places:

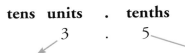

tens units . tenths

          3 . 5

The 3 has a value of three units.   The 5 has a value of five tenths.

▶ To multiply a number by 10, move the digits to the next highest place.

To work out 3.5 × 10, you move the digits to the next highest place:

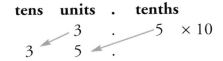

tens units . tenths

          3 . 5 × 10

      3 5 .

$3.5 \times 10 = 35$

You do not have to write 0 in the tenths place because there are no digits after it.

example

What number is 10 times larger than 4.7?

Move the digits to the next highest place:
$4.7 \times 10 = 47.0$ or 47

Check
$4 \times 10 = 40$
$5 \times 10 = 50$
so 4.7×10 is between 40 and 50.

Exercise N3.3

1 Use the decimal point to write the length of each line.

Do not measure the lines.

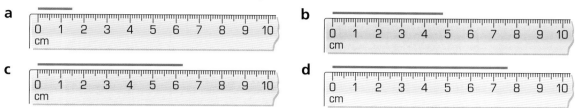

2 For each number, write down the value of the bold digit.
The first one is done for you.
   a 4.**9**   The 9 has a value of 9 tenths
   b 7.**2**   **c** 2**3**.8   **d** 32.5   **e** 45.**3**
   f 12**2**.6   **g** **5**21.9   **h** 527.**1**   **i** 345.**6**

3 Multiply these numbers by 10.
   a 5.8   **b** 2.7   **c** 7.1   **d** 9.9   **e** 3.3   **f** 4.3

4 Multiply these harder numbers by 10.
   a 15.2   **b** 12.3   **c** 11.1   **d** 13.9   **e** 18.3   **f** 24.2

5 These are the times that the Year 7 athletics team take to run
one lap of the school sports field.
Calculate the estimated times taken for each runner to finish 10 laps.

Runner	Time for one lap	Time for 10 laps
Mat	3.6 minutes	36 minutes
Claire	2.9 minutes	
Sarah	10.1 minutes	
Dinesh	13.3 minutes	
Lizzie	4.5 minutes	

6 The answer to 7.4 × 10 will be more than 70 and less than 80.
Choose the pair of numbers these answers should lie between.
   a 6.8 × 10:   50 and 60   or   60 and 70
   b 2.9 × 10:   30 and 40   or   20 and 30
   c 13.2 × 10:   30 and 40   or   130 and 140
   d 19.8 × 10:   190 and 200   or   20 and 30

This spread will show you how to:

▶▶ Divide whole numbers by 10 and explain the effect.

KEYWORDS
Place value
Divide
Tenths

You can use a calculator to divide by 10:

$50 \div 10 = 5$

Press: 5 0 ÷ 1 0 = ⎓ 5

> The digits move to the next lowest place.
>
> **hundreds   tens   units**
>
> 5 ⟍ 0
>
>   ⟍ 5

$170 \div 10 = 17$

Press: 1 7 0 ÷ 1 0 = ⎓ 17

> All the digits move to the next lowest place.
> The hundred moves to the tens place and the
> tens move to the units place:
>
> **hundreds   tens   units**
>
> 1 ⟍ 7 ⟍ 0
>
>   ⟍ 1   ⟍ 7

▶ To divide by 10, move the digits to the next lowest place.

Tenths is the first decimal place.

The next lowest place after the units is the tenths.

example

Work out:

a $24 \div 10$

b $75 \div 10$

a tens   units . tenths

2 ⟍ 4 ⟍

   ⟍ 2 . ⟍ 4

$24 \div 10 = 2.4$

b tens   units . tenths

7 ⟍ 5 ⟍

   ⟍ 7 . ⟍ 5

$75 \div 10 = 7.5$

Exercise N3.4

1 Divide these whole numbers by 10.
   a 60   **b** 80   **c** 50   **d** 40   **e** 20   **f** 100
   g 130   **h** 170   **i** 190   **j** 210   **k** 360   **l** 400

2 These pipelines are made from smaller pipes.
   Each of the smaller pipes is 10 m long.

   How many smaller pipes are needed to make each pipeline?

a

— 60 m —

b

— 110 m —

c

— 220 m —

d

— 480 m —

3 The picture shows £30. There are three £10 notes.
   How many £10 notes are needed to make these sums of money?
   a £50   **b** £60   **c** £90   **d** £150   **e** £180
   f £300   **g** £500   **h** £700   **i** £750   **j** £780

4 Divide these numbers by 10.
   Make your decimal points clear.
   a $56 \div 10 =$ **b** $23 \div 10 =$ **c** $15 \div 10 =$ **d** $46 \div 10 =$

5 When you divide units by 10 your answers will be decimals.
   You move the digits to the next lowest place.

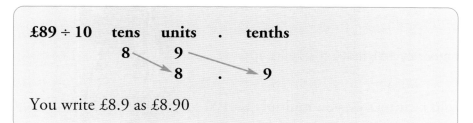

   You write £8.9 as £8.90

   Divide these amounts by 10. Write your answers in money.
   a £18 ÷ 10 =   **b** £42 ÷ 10 =   **c** £79 ÷ 10 =
   d £72 ÷ 10 =   **e** £80 ÷ 10 =   **f** £45 ÷ 10 =

This spread will show you how to:
▶▶ Multiply and divide numbers by 10.
▶▶ Convert from larger to smaller units.

On a ruler, a centimetre is divided into 10 smaller units.

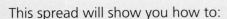

You can use cm and mm as shorthand for centimetres and millimetres.

The smaller units are called millimetres.

▶ **1 centimetre = 10 millimetres**

To convert centimetres to millimetres, you multiply by 10.

▶ **To multiply a number by 10, move the digits to the next highest place.**

example

Convert 12 cm into millimetres.

You multiply 12 by 10.

hundreds	**tens**	**units**
	1	2
1	2	0

So 12 cm = 120 mm

A tall person measures about 1.9 metres.

▶ **1 metre = 100 centimetres**

▶ **To multiply a number by 100, move the digits up two higher places.**

To convert 1.9 m into centimetres, you multiply by 100.

hundreds	**tens**	**units**	**.**	**tenths**
		1	.	9
1	9	0		

You add a zero in the units place.

1.9 m = 190 cm

Exercise N3.5

1 Multiply these numbers by 10.

   a $5 \times 10 =$ **b** $9 \times 10 =$ **c** $6 \times 10 =$ **d** $8 \times 10 =$

   e $13 \times 10 =$ **f** $15 \times 10 =$ **g** $21 \times 10 =$ **h** $32 \times 10 =$

2 Convert these centimetre lengths into millimetres.

   a 4 cm = __ mm   **b** 2 cm = __ mm   **c** 7 cm = __ mm

   d 1 cm = __ mm   **e** 5 cm = __ mm   **f** 10 cm = __ mm

3 Re-write the measurements of this matchbox using millimetres.

   length = __ mm

   width = __ mm

   height = __ mm

4 This piece of string is 110 mm long.

   Write its length in cm.

> To convert mm to cm you divide by 10.

5 To convert metres into centimetres, you multiply by 100.

   Convert these metre distances into centimetres.

   a 4 m = __ cm   **b** 8 m = __ cm   **c** 6 m = __ cm

   d 2 m = __ cm   **e** 7 m = __ cm   **f** 5 m = __ cm

6 Convert these millimetre lengths into centimetres.

   a 20 mm = __ cm   **b** 50 mm = __ cm   **c** 90 mm = __ cm

   d 80 mm = __ cm   **e** 70 mm = __ cm   **f** 10 mm = __ cm

7 To convert centimetres into metres, you divide by 100.

   You move the digits two lower places:

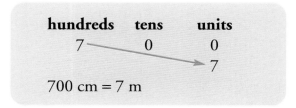

Convert these cm distances into metres.

   a 200 cm = __ m   **b** 400 cm = __ m   **c** 800 cm = __ m

   d 300 cm = __ m   **e** 600 cm = __ m   **f** 100 cm = __ m

This spread will show you how to:

▶▶ Partition.
▶▶ Use written methods for TU × U.

Roger can multiply two-digit numbers by one-digit numbers in his head.

To work out 16 × 9:

Multiply the 10 by the 9.
Then multiply the 6 by the 9.
Now add the two answers together.

He partitions the two-digit number into tens and units, then he multiplies each part.

He makes **jottings** to help keep track of his work.

16 × 9

10 × 9 = 90
 6 × 9 = 54

$$\begin{array}{r} 90 \\ + 54 \\ \hline 144 \end{array}$$

Here are his jottings for 13 × 6:

13 × 6

10 × 6 = 60
 3 × 6 = 18

$$\begin{array}{r} 60 \\ + 18 \\ \hline 78 \end{array}$$

He partitioned 13 into 10 and 3.

Exercise N3.6

1 Write down the answers to these questions.

  a $3 \times 9 =$ **b** $9 \times 3 =$ **c** $4 \times 7 =$

  d $5 \times 8 =$ **e** $6 \times 6 =$ **f** $8 \times 7 =$

  g $9 \times 4 =$ **h** $6 \times 3 =$ **i** $9 \times 8 =$

  j $7 \times 7 =$ **k** $5 \times 10 =$ **l** $4 \times 4 =$

Here is a multiplication table:

×	1	2	3	4	5	6	7	8	9	10
1	1	2	3	4	5	6	7	8	9	10
2	2	4	6	8	10	12	14	16	18	20
3	3	6	9	12	15	18	21	24	27	30
4	4	8	12	16	20	24	28	32	36	40
5	5	10	15	20	25	30	35	40	45	50
6	6	12	18	24	30	36	42	48	54	60
7	7	14	21	28	35	42	49	56	63	70
8	8	16	24	32	40	48	56	64	72	80
9	9	18	27	36	45	54	63	72	81	90
10	10	20	30	40	50	60	70	80	90	100

2 Copy and complete these calculations.
Try to do them from memory.

  a $4 \times \underline{\ \ } = 24$ **b** $9 \times \underline{\ \ } = 45$ **c** $7 \times \underline{\ \ } = 63$

  d $6 \times \underline{\ \ } = 36$ **e** $3 \times \underline{\ \ } = 27$ **f** $\underline{\ \ } \times 8 = 64$

  g $\underline{\ \ } \times 9 = 81$ **h** $10 \times \underline{\ \ } = 70$ **i** $4 \times \underline{\ \ } = 28$

3 Partition these numbers.
The first one is done for you.

  a 15: 10 and 5

  b 17   **c** 19   **d** 11   **e** 13

4 Partition these numbers.
The first one is done for you.

  a 24: 20 and 4

  b 27   **c** 31   **d** 35   **e** 42

  f 29   **g** 55   **h** 64   **i** 72

5 Partition these numbers and then multiply them.
Use jottings if it helps.

  a $13 \times 6 =$ **b** $15 \times 5 =$ **c** $19 \times 4 =$ **d** $18 \times 6 =$

  e $14 \times 6 =$ **f** $17 \times 6 =$ **g** $13 \times 8 =$ **h** $16 \times 8 =$

6 These problems have more than one ten.
Multiply the numbers. The first one is done for you.

  a 21×6: $20 \times 6 = 10 \times 6 \times 2 = 120$

                  $1 \times 6 = 6$

      so $21 \times 6 = 120 + 6 = 126$

  b $23 \times 4 =$ **c** $27 \times 4 =$ **d** $26 \times 5 =$ **e** $24 \times 6 =$

7 There are 33 matches in a box.
How many matches are there in 7 boxes?

This spread will show you how to:

▶▶ Use informal written methods for division.

KEYWORDS
Divide
Division

Number lines can help you to divide.

To work out $28 \div 4$:

Start at 0. ➡ Jump in steps of 4 until you reach 28.

You could start at 28 and jump backwards until you reach 0:

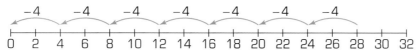

There are 7 jumps, so $28 \div 4 = 7$

Your number line doesn't have to be accurate.

To work out $32 \div 8$:

Until you reach 0. ⬅ Jump backwards in steps of 8. ⬅ Start at 32.

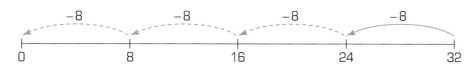

Number the position that you jump to each time.

There are 4 jumps of 8 from 32 to 0, so $32 \div 8 = 4$

example

Divide: $48 \div 16$.

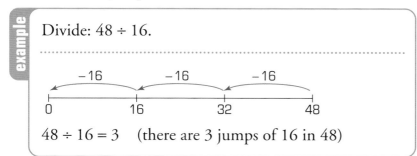

$48 \div 16 = 3$ (there are 3 jumps of 16 in 48)

Exercise N3.7

1 Use number lines to divide these numbers.
   a 12 ÷ 4 =   b 18 ÷ 6 =   c 18 ÷ 2 =
   d 16 ÷ 8 =   e 24 ÷ 8 =   f 28 ÷ 7 =
   g 26 ÷ 2 =   h 32 ÷ 4 =   i 32 ÷ 8 =
   j 28 ÷ 2 =   k 25 ÷ 5 =   l 22 ÷ 2 =

2 Use a number line to help you to solve these division
   problems.
   a How many 5 ml spoons of medicine can be taken from
      a bottle containing 35 ml?
   b How many 5 ml spoonfuls can you take from a bottle
      that contains 50 ml?

3 How many times can you subtract 5 from 60?

4 Use number line sketches to work out these divisions.
   The first one is done for you.
   a 60 ÷ 15

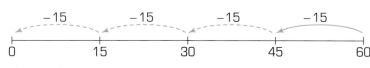

   60 ÷ 15 = 4

   b 36 ÷ 6 =   c 35 ÷ 5 =   d 40 ÷ 8 =
   e 27 ÷ 9 =   f 66 ÷ 6 =   g 52 ÷ 4 =
   h 60 ÷ 4 =   i 51 ÷ 3 =   j 72 ÷ 6 =

5 These calculations need jumps that are larger than 10.
   Sketch number lines to help you work them out.
   a 39 ÷ 13 =   b 45 ÷ 15 =   c 75 ÷ 15 =   d 56 ÷ 14 =

6 A minibus holds 16 people.
   How many minibuses do you need to carry
   64 supporters to a soccer match?

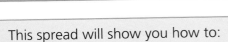

This spread will show you how to:
- Use doubling or halving.
- Use informal written methods for division.

KEYWORDS

Divide   Half

Subtract   Double

Joel can divide some numbers by doubling or halving.

40 ÷ 5 = 8,
so
80 ÷ 5 = 16
because
80 is double 40

48 ÷ 12 = 4
To divide 48 by 6
you double 4 because
6 is half of 12.
48 ÷ 6 = 8
  half double

For harder numbers, you can divide by repeating subtraction.
To work out 28 ÷ 7:

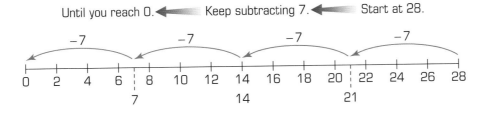

Until you reach 0. ← Keep subtracting 7. ← Start at 28.

You can write it like this:

$$28 - 7 = 21 \quad ... (1)$$
$$21 - 7 = 14 \quad ... (2)$$
$$14 - 7 = 7 \quad ... (3)$$
$$7 - 7 = 0 \quad ... (4)$$
$$\text{So } 28 \div 7 = 4$$

example

Work out:

a 36 ÷ 9   **b** 24 ÷ 8   **c** 39 ÷ 13

a Subtract 9.
$$36 - 9 = 27 \quad ... (1)$$
$$27 - 9 = 18 \quad ... (2)$$
$$18 - 9 = 9 \quad ... (3)$$
$$9 - 9 = 0 \quad ... (4)$$
So 36 ÷ 9 = 4

b Subtract 8.
$$24 - 8 = 16 \quad ... (1)$$
$$16 - 8 = 8 \quad ... (2)$$
$$8 - 8 = 0 \quad ... (3)$$
So 24 ÷ 8 = 3

c Subtract 13.
$$39 - 13 = 26 \quad ... (1)$$
$$26 - 13 = 13 \quad ... (2)$$
$$13 - 13 = 0 \quad ... (3)$$
So 39 ÷ 13 = 3

Exercise N3.8

1 Use the multiplication table on page 111 to help you work these out.
- **a** How many threes are there in 24?
- **b** How many fives are there in 40?
- **c** How many sixes are there in 30?
- **d** How many eights are there in 32?
- **e** How many sevens are there in 35?
- **f** How many nines are there in 72?
- **g** How many fours are there in 36?
- **h** How many fives are there in 40?
- **i** How many eights are there in 56?
- **j** How many sevens are there in 49?

2 Use doubling to copy and complete these divisions.
The first one is done for you.

- **a** $32 \div 4 = 8$
  so $64 \div 4 = 16$
- **b** $30 \div 5 = 6$
  so $60 \div 5 = \underline{\ \ }$
- **c** $24 \div 8 = 3$
  so $48 \div 5 = \underline{\ \ }$
- **d** $16 \div 4 = 4$
  so $32 \div 4 = \underline{\ \ }$
- **e** $27 \div 3 = 3$
  so $54 \div 3 = \underline{\ \ }$
- **f** $14 \div 2 = 7$
  so $28 \div 2 = \underline{\ \ }$

3 Use halving to copy and complete these divisions.
The first one is done for you.

- **a** $32 \div 4 = 8$
  so $32 \div 8 = 4$
- **b** $30 \div 5 = 6$
  so $30 \div 10 = \underline{\ \ }$
- **c** $18 \div 3 = 6$
  so $18 \div 6 = \underline{\ \ }$
- **d** $24 \div 4 = 6$
  so $24 \div 8 = \underline{\ \ }$
- **e** $36 \div 6 = 6$
  so $36 \div 12 = \underline{\ \ }$
- **f** $40 \div 4 = 10$
  so $40 \div 8 = \underline{\ \ }$

4
- **a** There are 40 sweets altogether in 5 jars.
  How many sweets are there in one jar?
- **b** There are 80 sweets in the 5 jars.
  How many sweets are there in one jar?
- **c** How many sweets are there in one jar
  if there are 160 sweets altogether?

5 Use subtraction to calculate these divisions.
- **a** $42 \div 6 =$
- **b** $49 \div 7 =$
- **c** $63 \div 7 =$
- **d** $64 \div 8 =$
- **e** $56 \div 7 =$
- **f** $35 \div 7 =$
- **g** $45 \div 9 =$
- **h** $72 \div 9 =$

6 Use subtraction to calculate these divisions.
- **a** $48 \div 16 =$
- **b** $64 \div 16 =$
- **c** $65 \div 13 =$
- **d** $52 \div 13 =$
- **e** $75 \div 15 =$
- **f** $63 \div 21 =$
- **g** $84 \div 21 =$
- **h** $105 \div 15 =$

7 To win a board game you have to reach 96.
If you can only move in steps of 12, how many steps will it
take to finish the game?

You should know how to ...

1 Use tenths written as a decimal.

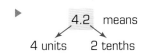

> 4.2 means
>
> 4 units 2 tenths

2 Multiply by 10 and understand the effect.
> ▶ You move the digits one place to the left:
>
> 59 × 10

hundreds	tens	units
	5	9
5	9	0

3 Round whole numbers to the nearest 10 or 100.
> ▶ 26 is nearer 30 than 20:
>
> 26
>
> 20   25   30
>
> 26 is 30 to the nearest 10.

4 Use all four operations to solve simple word problems.

Check out

1 Write a decimal number between 3.4 and 3.5.

2 A 10 litre can of paint costs £20.
What will it cost to buy these amounts
of paint?
a 20 litres
b 30 litres
c 50 litres
d 70 litres
e 90 litres

3 Round these distances from Penzance to:
a the nearest 100 miles
b the nearest 10 miles.

Aberdeen	660 miles
Edinburgh	542 miles
Fort William	650 miles
Kendal	403 miles
Leeds	375 miles

4 **a** A small potato weighs about 25 g.
Roughly how much do 10 small potatoes
weigh?
How many times heavier than one small
potato is a 1 kg large potato?
b A chocolate bar costs 19p.
How many bars can you buy for £5?

This unit will show you how to:

▶▶ Use doubling and halving, starting from known facts.

▶▶ Know multiplication facts by heart.

▶▶ Recognise multiples.

▶▶ Use the link between multiplication and division.

▶▶ Know squares of numbers.

▶▶ Find all the pairs of factors of a number.

▶▶ Begin to use ideas of simple proportion.

▶▶ Read and plot coordinates in the first quadrant.

▶▶ Recognise and extend number sequences.

▶▶ Explain methods and reasoning.

You can describe how plants grow using a mapping.

Before you start

You should know how to ...

1 Recognise multiples of 2, 5 and 10.

2 Recognise positions.

3 Recognise rectangles and squares.

Check in

1 Which of these numbers are multiples of 5?

20	5	52	25

2 Write down the coordinates of each letter on this grid:

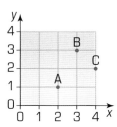

3 Name these shapes.

a    b

This spread will show you how to:

▶▶ Use doubling and halving, starting from known facts.
▶▶ Know multiplication facts by heart.

KEYWORDS

Factor	Row
Times table	Multiply
Double	Halve

This multiplication table shows the times tables up to 10×10.

×	1	2	3	4	5	6	7	8	9	10
1	1	2	3	4	5	6	7	8	9	**10**
2	2	4	6	8	**10**	12	14	16	18	20
3	3	6	9	12	15	18	21	24	27	30
4	4	8	12	16	20	24	28	32	36	40
5	5	**10**	15	20	25	30	35	40	45	50
6	6	12	18	24	30	36	42	48	54	60
7	7	14	21	28	35	42	49	56	63	70
8	8	16	24	32	40	48	56	64	72	80
9	9	18	27	36	45	54	63	72	81	90
10	**10**	20	30	40	50	60	70	80	90	100

The number 10 appears four times:

$10 = 1 \times 10$ and $10 = 10 \times 1$
$10 = 2 \times 5$ and $10 = 5 \times 2$.

The numbers that multiply together to make 10 are: 1, 2, 5 and 10.
These are the factors of 10.

You can think of factors like the number of counters in a row.

You can arrange 10 counters in rows in four different ways:

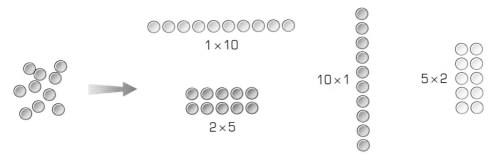

1×10

2×5

10×1

5×2

▶ The factors of 10 are: 1, 2, 5 and 10.

Exercise A3.5

1 This graph shows the before and after heights of plants after Clegg's FastGro treatment.

  a Use the graph to copy and complete this mapping:

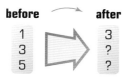

before → **after**

before	after
1	3
3	?
5	?

  b Use the graph to find the height of a 2 m plant after feeding with Clegg's FastGro.

  c Use the graph to find the height of a 4 m plant after feeding with Clegg's FastGro.

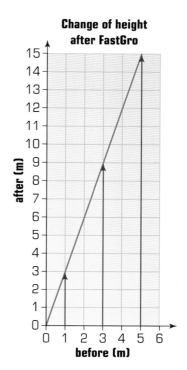

Change of height after FastGro

after (m) vs *before (m)*

2 There is another product called TruGrow.
The before and after heights after TruGrow feeding are shown on this graph.

  a Use the graph to complete this mapping of values:

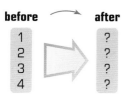

before → **after**

before	after
1	?
2	?
3	?
4	?

  b What is the factor that links the height of the plants before and after feeding?

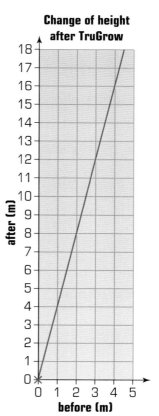

Change of height after TruGrow

after (m) vs *before (m)*

3 Imagine that the graph in question 2 is extended.

  a How tall would a 6 m plant be after feeding?

  b If a plant was 20 m after feeding, estimate how tall it was before feeding.

A3.6 Mappings and graphs

This spread will show you how to:

▶▶ Read and plot coordinates in the first quadrant.
▶▶ Recognise and extend number sequences.

KEYWORDS

Coordinates	Grid
Axes	Mapping
Value	Plot
Straight line	Graph

Plotting coordinates

▶ Coordinates give the exact location of a point on a grid.

The red cross is at coordinates (1, 2).
The green cross is at coordinates (4, 6).
The blue cross is at coordinates (7, 2).

The axes are called $x \rightarrow$ and $y \uparrow$.

▶ To plot coordinates, you count across first then up or down.

The *x*-axis is across and the *y*-axis is up or down.

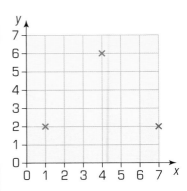

You number the lines, **not** the squares.

Drawing graphs of mappings

This mapping shows that the *y*-values are 4 more than the *x*-values.

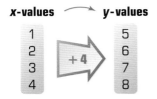

x-values   **y-values**

You plot the pairs of values as coordinates:

x-coordinate	*y*-coordinate
(1,	5)
(2,	6)
(3,	7)
(4,	8)

You join the points to make a graph.

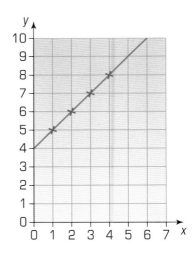

The points make a **straight line** because the *y*-coordinate is always 4 more than the *x*-coordinate.

Exercise A3.6

1 a Draw two coordinate grids like this one.
  b Label the *x*-axis **x** and the *y*-axis **y**.
  c Number the grid lines like these.

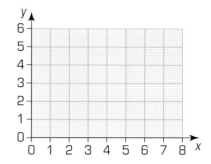

2 a On your first grid, plot these coordinates:
    (2, 2)   (2, 6)   (6, 6)   (6, 2)   (2, 2)
  b Join the points together with straight lines.
  c What shape have you made?

3 a On your second grid, plot these points:
    (2, 1)   (6, 1)   (8, 3)   (6, 5)   (1, 5)   (2, 1)
  b Join the coordinates with straight lines.
  c How many sides does the new shape have?

4 This picture shows how a fence is made.
The posts are linked by chains.

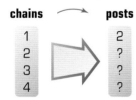

2 posts   3 posts   4 posts

1 chain   2 chains   3 chains

  a Copy and continue the pattern to show the link
    between the posts and chains on a mapping.

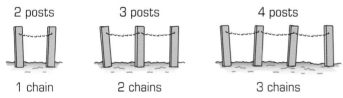

chains → **posts**

chains	posts
1	2
2	?
3	?
4	?

  b Write the mapping values as coordinates:
    (1, 2) ...
  c Plot the coordinates onto a grid like this.
  d Join the points to make a straight line.
  e How do you calculate the number of posts if you
    know the number of chains?

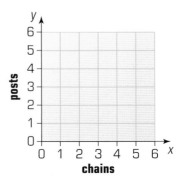

You should know how to ...

1 Recognise multiples.

  ▶ Multiples are numbers in a multiplication table.
  ▶ The multiples of 3 are:
     3, 6, 9, 12, 15, ...

2 Find all the factor pairs of a number.

  ▶ The factor pairs of 10 are:
     1 and 10, 2 and 5

3 Read and plot coordinates in the first quadrant.

Check out

1 Which of the numbers in the box are multiples of 4?

5	8	20	26
32	38	42	50

2 Find all the factor pairs of 30.

3 Plot these pairs of values on a copy of the grid.

(1,2)   (3, 6)   (4, 8)

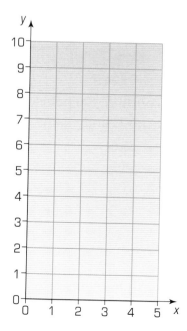

Exercise N4.5

1 What is the ratio of paint used in each mixture?

a

blue : yellow =

b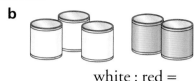

white : red =

c

red : blue =

d

white : black =

2 What is the ratio of green beads to blue beads on each string?

a

b

c

d

3 a Carl mixes paint in the ratio 2 tins of yellow to 1 tin of red.

> The ratio is 2 : 1.

He has 5 tins of red paint.
How many tins of yellow paint will he need?

b Carl mixes paint in the ratio 3 tins of yellow to 1 tin of blue.

> The ratio is 3 : 1.

He has 9 tins of yellow paint.
How many tins of blue paint will he need?

4 The ratio of red beads to yellow beads is 3 : 1 .

a You have 12 red beads.
How many yellow beads do you need?

b You have 5 yellow beads.
How many red beads do you need?

5 The ratio of black beads to red beads is 5 : 2 .

a You have 10 black beads.
How many red beads do you need?

b You have 6 red beads.
How many black beads do you need?

You should know how to ...

1 Write fractions as a division.

▶ To find $\frac{1}{2}$ you divide by 2.

$\frac{1}{2}$ of 4 = 4 ÷ 2 = 2

▶ To find $\frac{1}{3}$ you divide by 3.

$\frac{1}{3}$ of 9 = 9 ÷ 3 = 3

2 Read and write tenths and hundredths as decimals.

3.64

means 3 units   6 tenths   4 hundredths

3 Write fractions as a decimal.

▶ $\frac{23}{100} = 0.23$

4 Find simple percentages of whole number quantities.

▶ 50% means $\frac{50}{100} = \frac{1}{2}$

▶ 100% means $\frac{10}{100} = \frac{1}{10}$

Check out

1 Find:

a $\frac{1}{2}$ of 12

b $\frac{1}{2}$ of 18

c $\frac{1}{3}$ of 12

d $\frac{1}{3}$ of 15

2 Write down the decimal number that each arrow points to.

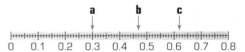

3 Write these as a decimal number:

a $\frac{15}{100}$

b $\frac{19}{100}$

c $\frac{52}{100}$

d $\frac{60}{100}$

4 Find:
  a 10% of £30.
  b 50% of 200 g.
  c 25% of £100.

This unit will show you how to:

▶▶ Make general statements about numbers.

▶▶ Understand the links between the four operations and how to do and undo them.

▶▶ Use symbols to compare numbers.

▶▶ Check results using inverse operations.

▶▶ Explain methods and reasoning.

Solving an equation is about balancing both sides.

Before you start

You should know how to ...

1 Do mental additions effectively by adding in any order.

2 Compare and order numbers.

Check in

1 Work out in your head:

  a 7 + 24

  b 6 + 19

  c 8 + 47

  d 9 + 35

2 Write these numbers in order of size, starting with the smallest:

17	6	31	12	9

This spread will show you how to:
▶▶ Make general statements about numbers.

KEYWORDS
Letter   Unknown
Altogether   Metres
Centimetres

There are a lot of sweets in the machine.
Geena takes 5 of them out.

I wonder how many are left?

We don't know how many there were at the start.

Let's say the number of sweets in the machine was **n**. We don't know **n**, but we know that there are 5 sweets less than **n** left.

So that means there are:
n − 5
sweets left!

▶ You can use letters to stand for unknown numbers.

This is the straw that broke the camel's back.

Call the number on the camel's back s.

One more broke its back.

Now you can write how many straws there were altogether.

The number of straws that broke its back is s + 1.

Exercise A4.1

1 You can use a letter to stand for a number.

  a There are *n* sweets in the jar.
    Josh takes 10 sweets from the jar.
    How many sweets are left?
    Write: There are *n* − ____ sweets in the jar.

  b There are *m* sweets in another jar.
    Kiya puts an extra 6 sweets into the jar.
    How many sweets are in the jar now?

2 There are too many people to count.
Say that there are *x* people running.
x stands for the number of people.

  a How many people will there be if 2 more join
    the runners?

  b Say that there are *y* people running.
    How many will be left if 5 people leave
    the runners?

3 You do not know the length of this string.
Call it *a* centimetres long.
How long will it be after you cut off 50 centimetres?

4 Write down the total length of each of these pipes
when they are joined end-to-end.

  a
    n metres   15 metres

  b
    5 metres   *y* metres

  c
    12 metres   *s* metres   20 metres

  d
    n metres   *n* metres

This spread will show you how to:

▶▶ Understand the links between the four operations and how to do and undo them.

KEYWORDS
Inverse   Equals (=)
Operation

You can write equal amounts in different ways.

Addition and subtraction

You can write 8 as:

These are equalities.

▶ The amounts on both sides of an equals sign (=) have the same value.

$$3 + 5 = 5 + 3$$

Both sides of the equals sign have the value of 8.

You can undo an addition by a subtraction:

▶ Subtraction is the inverse of addition.

Multiplication and division

You can write 10 as 2×5 or as 5×2

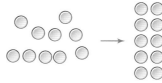
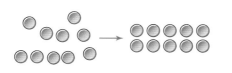

$2 \times 5 = 5 \times 2$ because both sides equal 10.

4 Transformations

This unit will show you how to:

▶▶ Recognise reflective symmetry in shapes.

▶▶ Reflect a shape in a mirror line.

▶▶ Translate a shape.

▶▶ Make clockwise and anticlockwise turns.

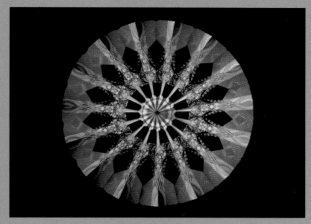

You can make beautiful patterns by reflecting shapes

Before you start

You should know how to …

1 Identify lines of symmetry in simple shapes.

2 Make and describe right-angled turns.

Check in

1 Which of these dotted lines are lines of symmetry? Answer Yes or No.

a   b

c   d

2 Describe each of these turns.
Choose your answer from this list:

| 90° | 180° | 360° |

a   b   c

This spread will show you how to:

▶▶ Recognise reflective symmetry in shapes.

KEYWORDS
Reflection   Symmetry
Line symmetry

Kelly folds a piece of card ...

... she cuts a shape along the folded edge ...

then unfolds it.

The fold line is a line of symmetry.

▶ A shape has line symmetry if it folds exactly onto itself.

These shapes have one line of symmetry:

The dashed line shows a line of symmetry.

These shapes have no lines of symmetry:

These shapes have more than one line of symmetry:

2 lines of symmetry

3 lines of symmetry

4 lines of symmetry

You can check for symmetry using a mirror:

Place a mirror along the line of symmetry.

The reflection completes the whole shape.

Exercise S4.1

1 Copy these shapes onto squared paper.
Complete the reflection and name the shape.

a

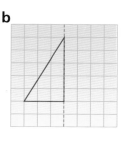 **b** 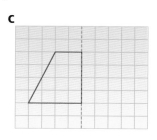 **c** 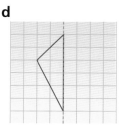 **d**

2 Copy these shapes and draw the line of symmetry.
These shapes have only one line of symmetry.

a  **b** 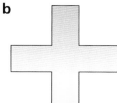 **c** **d** 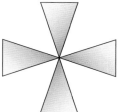 **e**

3 Copy these shapes and draw the lines of symmetry.
These shapes have more than one line of symmetry.

a **b** **c**

4 These shapes are all regular.
All the sides are equal in length and all the angles are equal.

a Find all the lines of symmetry of each shape.
b Write your results in a table like this:

What do you notice?

Number of sides	Number of lines of symmetry
3	
4	
5	
6	

S4.2 Reflection symmetry

This spread will show you how to:
▶▶ Reflect a shape in a mirror line.

KEYWORDS
Object   Image
Mirror line   Reflection

The object is in front of the mirror.

The object is further away.

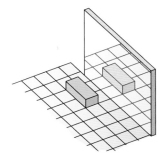 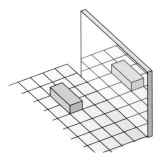

You can see the image in the mirror.

The image is further away too.

▶ A reflection is a mirror image.

You can reflect a shape in a mirror line on a grid:

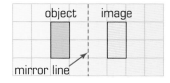 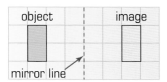

You can reflect shapes in more than one mirror line.

example

Reflect shape A in line X. Label it B.
Reflect shape A in line Y. Label it C.

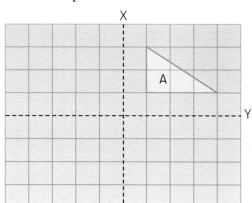 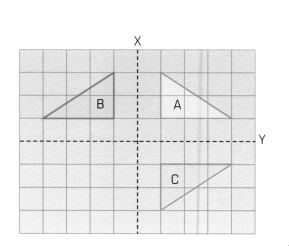

Exercise S4.2

1 This is Emma.
Which drawing shows her reflection when she is looking in a mirror?

Emma   the reflections

2 Copy each shape and mirror line onto squared paper.
Draw the reflection of the shape in the mirror line.

a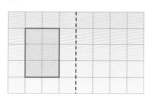

b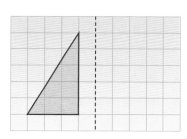

c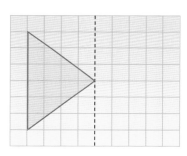

d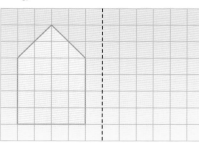

e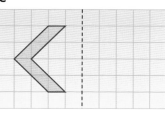

f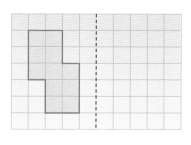

3 Copy this grid – it is 10 squares by 10 squares.
Copy the mirror lines A and B onto the grid.

  a Reflect the shape in mirror line A.
  b Reflect the shape in mirror line B.

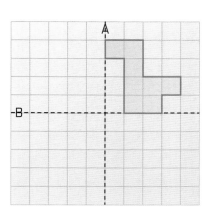

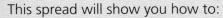

S4.3 Symmetry on a grid

This spread will show you how to:

⏩ Read and plot coordinates in the first quadrant.
⏩ Reflect a shape in a mirror line.

KEYWORDS

Reflect   Point
Mirror line   Shape
Reflection   Distance
Coordinates   Object

You can reflect a shape on a coordinate grid.

▶ To plot coordinates, you count across first then up.
(3, 2) means 3 across then 2 up.

The coordinates of the corners of the blue rectangle are:

The rectangle is reflected in the mirror line. The coordinates of the image are:

A (5, 2)
B (5, 5)
C (1, 5)
D (1, 2)

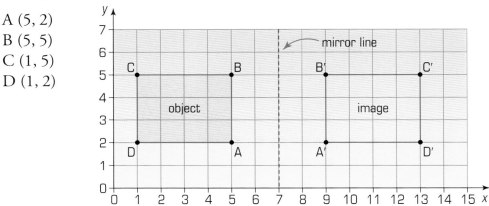

A′ (9, 2)
B′ (9, 5)
C′ (13, 5)
D′ (13, 2)

Each pair of points are the same distance from the mirror line.

▶ To reflect a shape, you reflect each point in the mirror line.

example

Reflect this object in the mirror line.
What does the complete drawing show?

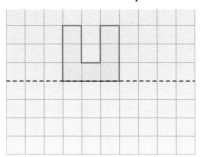

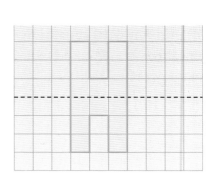

It's the letter H.

Exercise S4.3

1 Give the coordinates for each of the points:
D, E, F, G and H.

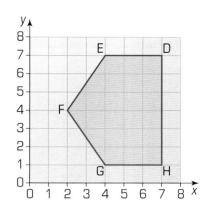

2 a Copy this grid and the mirror line.
  b Plot these points and join them to make a shape:
    A (6, 7)   B (3, 7)   C (5, 1).
  c Draw the reflection of the shape in the mirror line.
  d Give the coordinates of the reflected shape:
    A', B', C'.

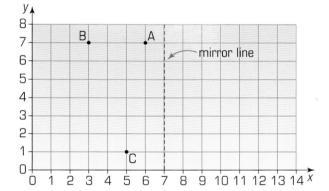

3 a Make another copy of the grid and mirror line in question 2.
  b Plot these points and join them to make a shape:
    R (5, 1)   S (5, 7)   T (3, 7)   U (3, 1).
  c Draw the reflection of the shape in the mirror line.
  d Give the coordinates of the reflected shape: R', S', T', U'.

4 a Copy this grid and the mirror line.
  b Plot and join these points to make a line:
    (7, 5) (5, 5).
  c Plot and join these points to make a triangle:
    (7, 9) (5, 7) (7, 7).
  d Plot and join these points to make a triangle:
    (3, 11) (4, 10) (6, 11).
  e Plot these points. Join them as you go.
    (7, 15) (5, 15) (3, 14) (2, 12) (1, 12)
    (1, 9) (2, 8) (3, 5) (6, 3) (7, 3).
  f Reflect all the points, lines and shapes in the mirror line.
    What have you drawn?

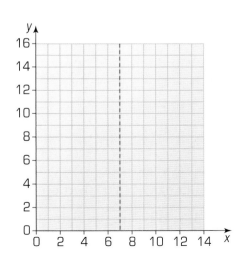

This spread will show you how to:

▶▶ Translate a shape.

KEYWORDS
Shape   Point
Translation Movement

A shape can move on a grid by sliding:

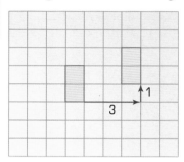

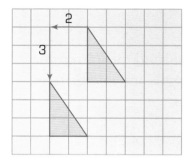

The rectangle moves:
3 squares right and 1 up

The triangle moves:
2 squares left and 3 down

This sliding movement is called a translation.

▶ In a translation, the shape moves:
  ▶ left or right first, then
  ▶ up or down.

Each point on the shape translates by the same amount.

example

The grid shows a shape and some translations.
Describe the translation that takes:
a A to B
b B to C
c A to C.

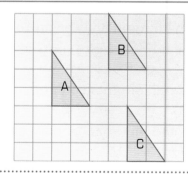

Count across first, then up or down.

a A to B is 3 to the right then 2 up.

b B to C is 1 to the right then 5 down.

c A to C is 4 to the right then 3 down.

Exercise S4.4

1 Copy and complete these statements to describe each translation.

a ___ to the right.
___ up.

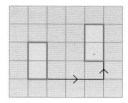

b ___ to the left.
___ down.

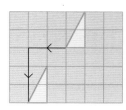

2 Each translation moves triangle A to another triangle.
Give the number of the triangle it moves to.

a 1 to the right and 3 up.

b 2 to the left and 2 down.

c 5 to the right and 4 down.

d 4 to the left and 6 up.

e 5 to the left and 6 down.

f 7 to the right and 4 up.

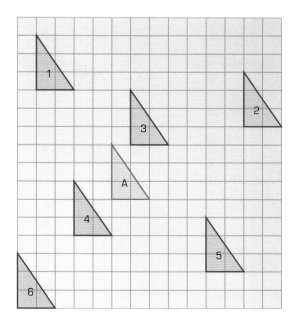

3 a Copy this 10 × 10 grid.
b Copy each of the shapes.
Draw them in place carefully.
c Move the red triangle 4 right and 2 down.
Label the new shape A.
d Move the green square 2 right and 5 up.
Label the new shape B.
e Move the blue rectangle 4 left and 3 down.
Label the new shape C.

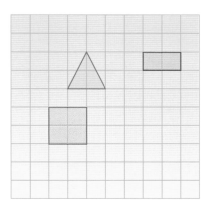

This spread will show you how to:

▶▶ Make clockwise and anticlockwise turns.

KEYWORDS
Turn   Angle
Rotation   Clockwise
Degrees (°)
Anticlockwise

This arrow is turning in a clockwise direction.

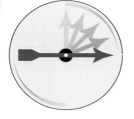

This arrow is turning in an anticlockwise direction.

▶ You measure turns in angles using degrees, ° for short.

This is a clockwise turn of 90°.

It is $\frac{1}{4}$ turn.

This is a clockwise turn of 180°.

It is $\frac{1}{2}$ turn.

This is a clockwise turn of 360°.

It is 1 turn.

This firework rotates about a fixed point:

▶ A rotation is a turn.

You can rotate a shape about a point to make a pattern.

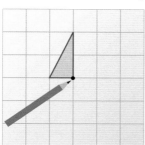

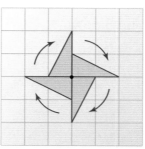

Use a pencil to keep the point in place.

Exercise S4.5

1 Choose the direction and angle from the boxes to describe each turn:

clockwise   anticlockwise

90°   180°   360°

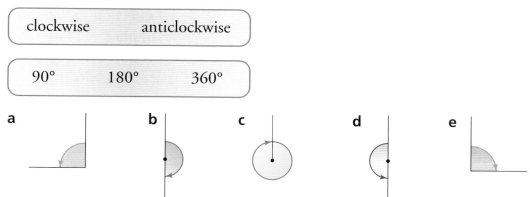

a   b   c   d   e

2 a Sketch this shape after it turns 90° anticlockwise about the dot.

b Sketch this shape after it turns 180° clockwise about the dot.

3 Sketch these letters after a rotation of 180° clockwise about the cross.

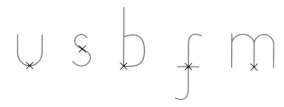

You can turn the page upside-down to see a 180° turn.

4 a Copy this shape on squared paper.
  b Rotate the shape about the dot clockwise through 90°.
  c Draw the rotated shape.
  d Rotate the shape through 90° again. Draw the rotated shape.
  e Repeat until the shape is back at the start.

You should have four shapes in your pattern.

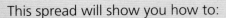
This spread will show you how to:
- ▶▶ Reflect a shape in a mirror line.
- ▶▶ Translate a shape.
- ▶▶ Make clockwise and anticlockwise turns.

KEYWORDS

Reflection	Mirror line
Distance	Rotation
Clockwise	Shape
Translation	Turn
Anticlockwise	

You can move a shape on a grid in different ways:

Reflection in a mirror line

▶ To reflect a shape, you reflect each point in the mirror line.

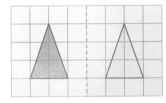

The shape is flipped over.

The shapes are the same distance from the mirror line.

Translation

A translation is a sliding movement.

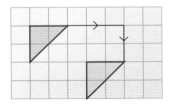

Translation of 3 right 2 down.

Each point moves the same distance.

▶ In a translation, the shape moves:
  - ▶ left or right first, then
  - ▶ up or down.

Rotation

▶ A rotation is a turn.

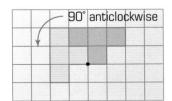

You rotate the shape about a point.

Exercise S4.6

1 Copy each shape onto squared paper.
Draw the reflection in the mirror line.

a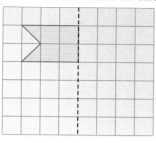
b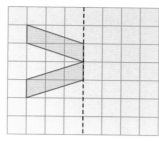
c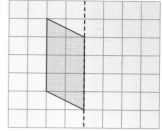

2 Copy each shape and mirror line onto squared paper.
Reflect each shape in the mirror line.

a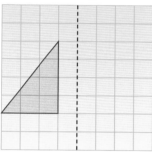
b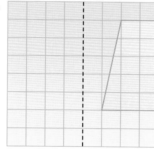
c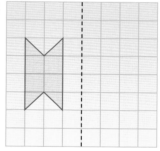

3 **a** Move the square 3 right and 2 down.
Which number will it land on?

b Describe this translation in words.

			8	
			2	10
			6	11
			4	9
1		13	5	7	3
	12		14	

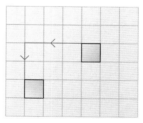

4 **Brainteaser**
The red cog turns in a
clockwise direction.
In which direction do
each of the other cogs
turn?

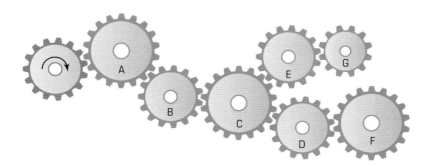

You should know how to ...

1 Recognise line symmetry in shapes.

▶ This shape has line symmetry.

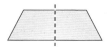

2 Reflect a shape in a mirror line.

▶ You reflect each point in the mirror line.

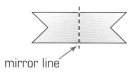

mirror line

3 Translate a shape.

▶ In a translation the shape moves:

▶ left or right first, then

▶ up or down.

Check out

1 Do these shapes have line symmetry?

a   b

2 Copy this shape onto squared paper and reflect it in the mirror line.

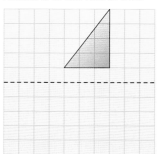

3 Describe how to translate the orange shape onto the blue shape.

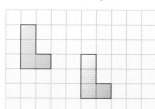

5 More number calculations

This unit will show you how to:

▶▶ Use words to explain estimation and approximation.

▶▶ Make and justify estimates.

▶▶ Use, read and write standard metric units.

▶▶ Round a number to the nearest whole numbers.

▶▶ Find all the pairs of factors of any number up to 100.

▶▶ Use factors to multiply mentally.

▶▶ Extend written methods to:
  ▶ short multiplication of HTU × U
  ▶ short division of HTU ÷ U.

▶▶ Recognise when two simple fractions are equivalent.

▶▶ Write fractions as a division.

▶▶ Use division to find simple fractions of amounts.

▶▶ Find simple percentages of quantities.

▶▶ Use all four operations to solve simple word problems.

The cost is £132. £132 ÷ 6 – that's £22 each!

You can use mental calculations to help solve problems.

Before you start

You should know how to ...

1 Multiply and divide numbers up to 10 × 10 quickly.

2 Estimate a simple fraction.

Check in

1 Write the answers to:

a 2 × 3	**b** 3 × 5	**c** 5 × 7
d 6 × 4	**e** 6 × 8	**f** 8 × 7
g 20 ÷ 4	**h** 36 ÷ 4	**i** 30 ÷ 5
j 18 ÷ 6	**k** 36 ÷ 6	**l** 40 ÷ 5

2 Estimate the fraction of each shape that is red:

a   b   c

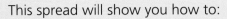

This spread will show you how to:

▶▶ Use words to explain estimation.
▶▶ Make and justify estimates.
▶▶ Use, read and write standard metric units.

KEYWORDS
Measure   Metre
Centimetre   Kilometre
Estimate

You can measure lengths using metric units:

Centimetres, cm for short

1 cm is about the width of a little finger.

Metres, m for short

1 m is about half the height of a door.

Kilometres, km for short

1 km takes about 20 minutes to walk.

The ruler is 1 metre or 100 cm long.
You can estimate the length of the snake.

It is less than 50 cm.
The snake is about 40 cm long.

40 cm is not an exact measurement, so you say 'about' 40 cm.

Robert Wadlow was a giant.

In this picture he is 2.8 m tall.

His friend is a little more than half of Robert's height.

▶ His friend is more than 1.4 m.
▶ His friend is about 1.6 m tall.

▶ Estimation is not accurate measurement.
   You say 'about' to show it is an estimate.

Exercise N5.1

1 How tall is this house?
  a 200 metres   **b** 20 metres
  c 2 km   **d** 20 cm

2 How far is it from London to Glasgow?
  a 40 km   **b** 650 km
  c 450 m   **d** 1000 m

3 **a** The wingspan of a Boeing 747 is about 65 m.

64.4 m

Estimate the wingspan of the small aeroplane.

  b Explain how you made your estimate.

4 This London bus is just over 4 m high.
Use this measurement to estimate the height of each
arrow from the ground.

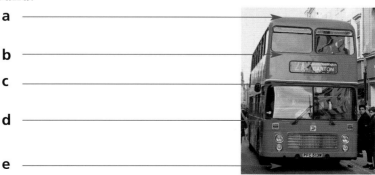

a

b

c

d

e

This spread will show you how to:

▶▶ Use words to explain approximation.
▶▶ Round a number with one decimal place to the nearest whole number.

KEYWORDS
Approximate
Approximation
Tonnes

You can round a decimal to the nearest whole number:

3.7 is between 3 and 4.
3.7 is nearer to 4.
3.7 rounds to 4.

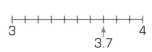

There are 5 cars on this lorry.

Each large car on the top weighs 1.8 tonnes.
Each small car on the bottom weighs 0.7 tonnes.

You can approximate the total weight of the cars:
▶ Round the decimal amounts:
   1.8 tonnes ≈ 2 tonnes
   0.7 tonnes ≈ 1 tonne
▶ Calculate using your approximation:
   The large cars weigh about   3 × 2 tonnes   = 6 tonnes.
   The small cars weigh about   2 × 1 tonne   = 2 tonnes.

The total weight is about 8 tonnes.

▶ To find an approximate answer, round the numbers first then calculate.

This picture measures 1.8 m by 1.4 m.
Find the approximate length of its perimeter.

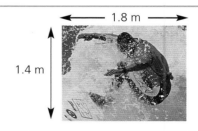

The perimeter is the distance around the shape.
Round the length and width:
   1.8 m ≈ 2 m   1.4 m ≈ 1 m
The perimeter is about 1 m + 2 m + 1 m + 2 m = 6 m.

Exercise N5.2

1 Round these amounts to the nearest whole unit.

    a 5.9 kg   **b** 10.2 kg   **c** 8.3 litres

    d 12.7 m   **e** 51.4 cm   **f** 0.5 m

    g 0.7 km   **h** £12.90   **i** 31.7 mm

    j 5.5 cm   **k** 0.2 litres   **l** 19.8 tonnes

2 The table shows how much Peter saved in six months.
Use rounding to work out an approximate total for his savings.
Give your answer to the nearest whole pound (£).

Week 1	Week 2	Week 3	Week 4	Week 5	Week 6
£3.50	£1.89	£6.20	£0.75	£1.00	£6.45

3 Find the approximate distance around the perimeter
of this hexagon.

Give your answer to the nearest centimetre.

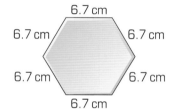

4 The red and green cars each weigh
0.6 tonnes.

The black car weighs 1.3 tonnes.
The silver cars weigh 1.7 tonnes.
The lorry weighs 8.3 tonnes.
Work out the approximate total
weight of all the vehicles.

5 a This rectangle measures 7.5 cm by 6.2 cm.
Find the approximate length of its perimeter.

   b The area of a rectangle = length × width.
Give an approximate answer for the area of the
rectangle.

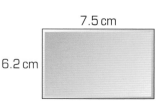

This spread will show you how to:
▶▶ Find all the factor pairs of a number to 100.
▶▶ Use factors to multiply mentally.

KEYWORDS
Factor   Multiply
Rectangle   Product

▶ Factors are numbers that multiply together to make a product.
$3 \times 6 = 18$ so 3 and 6 are factors of 18.

You can find factors from a multiplication table.

×	1	2	3	4	5	6	7	8	9	10
1	1	2	3	4	5	6	7	8	9	10
2	2	4	6	8	10	12	14	16	18	20
3	3	6	9	12	15	18	21	24	27	30
4	4	8	12	16	20	24	28	32	36	40
5	5	10	15	20	25	30	35	40	35	50
6	6	12	18	24	30	36	42	48	54	60
7	7	14	21	28	35	42	49	56	63	70
8	8	16	24	32	40	48	56	64	72	80
9	9	18	27	36	45	54	63	72	81	90
10	10	20	30	40	50	60	70	80	90	100

$2 \times 9 = 18$
$3 \times 6 = 18$

$6 \times 3 = 18$

$9 \times 2 = 18$

▶ All numbers have 1 and themselves as factors:
$1 \times 18 = 18$ and $18 \times 1 = 18$

18 has six different factors: $1 \times 18 = 18$ $2 \times 9 = 18$ $3 \times 6 = 18$

You can break down the factors further.

$18 = 3 \times 6$ and $6 = 3 \times 2$
So $18 = 3 \times 3 \times 2$

or

$18 = 2 \times 9$ and $9 = 3 \times 3$
So $18 = 2 \times 3 \times 3$

You can use factors to help multiply numbers together.

example

Work out:
a 13×6
b 12×16

a $13 \times 3 \times 2$
   $= 39 \times 2$
   $= 78$

b $12 \times 2 \times 2 \times 2 \times 2$
   $= 24 \times 2 \times 2 \times 2$
   $= 48 \times 2 \times 2$
   $= 96 \times 2$
   $= 192$

Exercise N5.3

1 Find all the factors of these numbers.
List the factors in pairs.
The first one is done for you.

a 10: $10 = 2 \times 5$
$\quad\quad\ 10 = 1 \times 10$

b 15: 15 =   **c** 20   **d** 25   **e** 14

f 16   **g** 24   **h** 30   **i** 40

2

You can make two different rectangles using 6 cm squares.

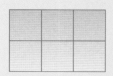 

The rectangles have these dimensions:

$3 \text{ cm} \times 2 \text{ cm} = 6 \text{ cm}^2$ $6 \text{ cm} \times 1 \text{ cm} = 6 \text{ cm}^2$

6 has four factors:

$3 \times 2 = 6$ $6 \times 1 = 6$

Rearrange these squares to make other rectangles.
Use your rectangles to list the factor pairs of each number.

a   **b**    **c**

3 Break these numbers down into factors.
The first one is done for you.

a 40: $40 = 4 \times 10$
    and $10 = 5 \times 2$
    so $40 = 4 \times 5 \times 2$

b 70   **c** 80   **d** 90   **e** 30   **f** 50

4 Use factors to help work out:

a 13×4 **b** 15×8 **c** 9×16 **d** 21×6

e 12×15 **f** 14×16 **g** 18×12 **h** 21×18

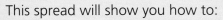
This spread will show you how to:

▶▶ Extend written methods to HTU × U.

You can partition larger numbers into place value parts:

		hundreds	tens	units	
24	means:		2	4	= 2 × 10 and 4 × 1
135	means:	1	3	5	= 1 × 100 and 3 × 10 and 5 × 1
762	means:	7	6	2	= 7 × 100 and 6 × 10 and 2 × 1

You can use jottings to keep track of your working.

example

John saves £13 a week for 7 weeks.
How much does he save altogether?

Partition 13 in a grid.

×	tens 10	units 3
7	70	21

$7 \times 3 = 21$

$7 \times 10 = 70$

$7 \times 13 = 7 \times 10 + 7 \times 3$
$= 70 + 21$
$= 91$

So John saved £91 altogether.

The grid is a useful way to work out harder multiplications.

example

Work out: 324 × 6.

Partition 324 into 300 + 20 + 4

×	hundreds 300	tens 20	units 4
6	1800	120	24

$324 \times 6 = 300 \times 6 + 20 \times 6 + 4 \times 6$
$= 1800 + 120 + 24$
$= 1944$

▶ To partition a number, split it into place value parts.

Exercise N5.4

1 Partition these numbers into hundreds, tens and units (ones).
The first one is done for you.

a $152 = 100 + 50 + 2$ **b** $29 = \_\_ + \_\_$

c $57 =$ **d** $98 =$ **e** $66 =$ **f** $70 =$

g $197 =$ **h** $150 =$ **i** $149 =$ **j** $238 =$

k $203 =$ **l** $580 =$ **m** $400 =$ **n** $309 =$

2 You can approximate before working out an answer.
This will help you to check your calculation:

> To approximate 29×3.
> ▶ Round: $29 \approx 30$
> ▶ Calculate: $30 \times 3 = 90$
> Expect your answer to be near to 90.

a Copy and complete this multiplication grid for 29×3:

×	20	
3		

b Is your answer close to the approximation of 90?

3 **a** Find an approximation of 58×6.

> Hint: 58 is very close to 60.

b Copy and complete this multiplication grid for 58×6:

×		8
6		

c Was your approximation more or less than the accurate answer?

4 For each of these multiplications:
- ▶ Find an approximation.
- ▶ Draw a grid and complete the calculation.
- ▶ Say if your approximation was near your accurate answer.

a 36×5 **b** 49×8 **c** 84×5 **d** 99×4

e 72×3 **f** 103×4 **g** 211×4 **h** 208×3

5 Henry buys 8 boxes of sweets.
There are 57 sweets in each box.

a Find an approximation of the number of sweets in 8 boxes.

b Use a grid to complete the calculation.

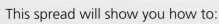

This spread will show you how to:

▶▶ Extend written methods to short division of HTU ÷ U.

KEYWORDS
Division   Multiplication
Jotting   Subtract

You can use multiplication tables to work out divisions.

This is part of the 3 times table.
You can use it to see how many times 3 divides into 27.

$9 \times 3 = 27$ so $27 \div 3 = 9$

It divides 9 times.

×	3
1	3
2	6
3	9
4	12
5	15
6	18
7	21
8	24
9	27
10	30

You can break larger divisions into smaller steps.
Using jottings will help you keep track of your working.

example

A wristband uses 3 beads.
Jo has 153 beads.
How many wrist bands can she make?

You need to work out $153 \div 3$.
You know that $10 \times 3 = 30$.

Subtract as many groups of $30 = 10 \times 3$ as you can:

$153 \div 3$

$$
\begin{array}{r}
1\ 5\ 3 \\
-\quad 3\ 0 \quad = 10 \times 3 \\
\hline
1\ 2\ 3 \\
-\quad 3\ 0 \quad = 10 \times 3 \\
\hline
9\ 3 \\
-\quad 3\ 0 \quad = 10 \times 3 \\
\hline
6\ 3 \\
-\quad 3\ 0 \quad = 10 \times 3 \\
\hline
3\ 3 \\
-\quad 3\ 0 \quad = 10 \times 3 \\
\hline
3 \\
-\quad 3 \quad = 1 \times 3 \\
\end{array}
$$

So there are:
$10 + 10 + 10 + 10 + 10 + 1 = 51$
groups of 3 in 153.
Jo can make 51 wrist bands.

Exercise N5.5

1 Copy and complete these multiplications.

   a $6 \times 10 =$ **b** $3 \times 10 =$ **c** $8 \times 10 =$

   d $5 \times 10 =$ **e** $7 \times 10 =$ **f** $9 \times 10 =$

   g $2 \times 10 =$ **h** $1 \times 10 =$

2 Divide these numbers.
You will need to jot down some working.
Follow the example on page 188.

   a $159 \div 3 =$ **b** $176 \div 4 =$ **c** $186 \div 6 =$

   d $234 \div 6 =$ **e** $255 \div 5 =$ **f** $176 \div 8 =$

   g $132 \div 4 =$ **h** $130 \div 5 =$ **i** $186 \div 3 =$

   j $279 \div 9 =$ **k** $288 \div 9 =$ **l** $328 \div 8 =$

> The answers in question 1 will help you.

3 Claire is making wristbands.
She uses 4 beads in each band.
She has 132 beads.
How many bands can she make?

4 Dinesh uses 3 scoops of ice cream for each dessert.
He has 142 scoops left in his freezer.
How many desserts will he be able to make?

5 A car needs 5 tyres.
A garage has 165 tyres in stock.
How many cars can be fitted?

6 Eggs are packed in boxes of 6.
How many boxes do you need to pack 312 eggs?

This spread will show you how to:

▶▶ Recognise when two simple fractions are equivalent.

KEYWORDS

Equivalent Quarter
Fraction   Divide
Half

This piece of cake has 4 equal squares.
Each square is a quarter, $\frac{1}{4}$ of the cake.

The cake is cut in half.
2 quarters of the cake is the same as half of the cake.

$\frac{2}{4}$ is the same as $\frac{1}{2}$.

▶ $\frac{2}{4}$ and $\frac{1}{2}$ are equivalent fractions.

In this 100 square:

30 squares are coloured green.

$\frac{30}{100}$ is green.

There are 10 strips.

3 strips are green.

$\frac{3}{10}$ is green.

$\frac{30}{100}$ and $\frac{3}{10}$ are equivalent: they show the same amount.

1	2	3	4	5	6	7	8	9	10
11	12	13	14	15	16	17	18	19	20
21	22	23	24	25	26	27	28	29	30
31	32	33	34	35	36	37	38	39	40
41	42	43	44	45	46	47	48	49	50
51	52	53	54	55	56	57	58	59	60
61	62	63	64	65	66	67	68	69	70
71	72	73	74	75	76	77	78	79	80
81	82	83	84	85	86	87	88	89	90
91	92	93	94	95	96	97	98	99	100

▶ Equivalent fractions show the same amount.

Exercise N5.6

1 Look at each pair of shapes.
Which pairs of fractions are equivalent to each other?

a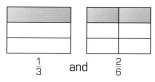
$\frac{1}{3}$ and $\frac{2}{6}$

b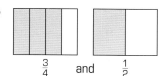
$\frac{3}{4}$ and $\frac{1}{2}$

c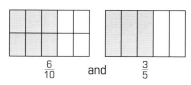
$\frac{6}{10}$ and $\frac{3}{5}$

d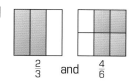
$\frac{2}{3}$ and $\frac{4}{6}$

e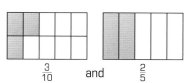
$\frac{3}{10}$ and $\frac{2}{5}$

f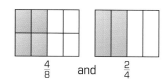
$\frac{4}{8}$ and $\frac{2}{4}$

2 Copy and complete the equivalent fraction pairs.
Count the dots in each fraction to help you.

a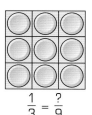
$\frac{1}{3} = \frac{?}{9}$

b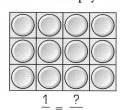
$\frac{1}{2} = \frac{?}{12}$

c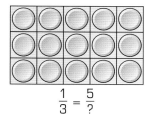
$\frac{1}{3} = \frac{5}{?}$

3 You can use multiplication and division to make equivalent fractions.
You multiply or divide both parts by the same number.

$$\frac{1}{2} \xrightarrow[\times 3]{\times 3} = \frac{3}{6} \qquad \frac{5}{10} \xrightarrow[\div 2]{\div 2} = \frac{1}{2}$$

Use multiplication or division to copy and complete these
pairs of equivalent fractions:

a $\frac{3}{4} = \frac{6}{?}$

b $\frac{1}{3} = \frac{?}{15}$

c $\frac{6}{10} = \frac{?}{5}$

d $\frac{2}{7} = \frac{4}{?}$

e $\frac{4}{10} = \frac{2}{?}$

f $\frac{10}{20} = \frac{?}{?}$

This spread will show you how to:

▶▶ Write fractions as a division.
▶▶ Use division to find simple fractions of amounts.

KEYWORDS

Divided	Fraction
Numerator	Quarter
Denominator	Half

▶ In the fraction $\dfrac{1}{4}$ — the numerator shows the number of parts you have
— the denominator shows the number of equal parts there are.

These 12 sheep are in 4 pens.
They are divided into quarters
(4 equal parts).

There are 3 sheep in each quarter:
$12 \div 4 = 3$

As a fraction you write:
$\frac{1}{4}$ of 12 = 3

▶ To find $\frac{1}{4}$ of an amount, you divide by 4.

▶ To find $\frac{1}{3}$ of an amount, you divide by 3.

▶ In the fraction $\dfrac{3}{4}$ — you have 3 parts.
— there are 4 equal parts.

Each quarter of 12 is 3.

So 3 quarters of 12 is 9.
$(3 \times 3 = 9)$

As a fraction you write $\frac{3}{4}$ of 12 = 9

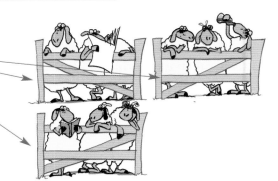

▶ $\frac{3}{4}$ of an amount is 3 lots of $\frac{1}{4}$ of the amount.

You divide by 4, then
multiply by 3.

Exercise N5.7

1 Calculate these fractions of amounts.
The multiplication table will help you.

a $\frac{1}{4}$ of 16 =   **b** $\frac{1}{4}$ of 20 =   **c** $\frac{1}{4}$ of 40 =

d $\frac{1}{4}$ of 36 =   **e** $\frac{1}{3}$ of 30 =   **f** $\frac{1}{3}$ of 15 =

g $\frac{1}{2}$ of 16 =   **h** $\frac{1}{2}$ of 20 =   **i** $\frac{1}{2}$ of 18 =

j $\frac{1}{5}$ of 50 =   **k** $\frac{1}{5}$ of 30 =   **l** $\frac{1}{5}$ of 15 =

m $\frac{1}{5}$ of 25 =   **n** $\frac{1}{4}$ of 24 =   **o** $\frac{1}{3}$ of 24 =

×	1	2	3	4	5
1	1	2	3	4	5
2	2	4	6	8	10
3	3	6	9	12	15
4	4	8	12	16	20
5	5	10	15	20	25
6	6	12	18	24	30
7	7	14	21	28	35
8	8	16	24	32	40
9	9	18	27	36	45
10	10	20	30	40	50

2 You can calculate fractions of some larger amounts by doubling.

> $\frac{1}{4}$ of 24 is 6,   so $\frac{1}{4}$ of 48 is 12   because 48 is double 24.
>
> $\frac{1}{3}$ of 30 is 10,   so $\frac{1}{3}$ of 60 is 20   because 60 is double 30.
>
> $\frac{1}{5}$ of 50 is 10,   so $\frac{1}{5}$ of 100 is 20   because 100 is double 50.

Use doubling to calculate these fractions of amounts.

a $\frac{1}{4}$ of 80 (Hint: find $\frac{1}{4}$ of 40 then double your answer.)

b $\frac{1}{4}$ of 72 (Hint: find $\frac{1}{4}$ of 36)   **c** $\frac{1}{4}$ of 64 (Hint: find $\frac{1}{4}$ of 32)

d $\frac{1}{4}$ of 56 (Hint: find $\frac{1}{4}$ of 28)   **e** $\frac{1}{5}$ of 90 (Hint: find $\frac{1}{5}$ of 45)

f $\frac{1}{3}$ of 36 (Hint: find $\frac{1}{3}$ of 18)   **g** $\frac{1}{5}$ of 80 (Hint: find $\frac{1}{5}$ of 40)

h $\frac{1}{5}$ of 70 (Hint: find $\frac{1}{5}$ of 35)   **i** $\frac{1}{3}$ of 48 (Hint: find $\frac{1}{3}$ of 24)

3 Calculate these fractions of amounts.
Use your answers to question 1 to help you.

a $\frac{3}{4}$ of 16 cm (Hint: $\frac{1}{4}$ of 16 = 4)

b $\frac{3}{4}$ of 20 kg =   **c** $\frac{3}{4}$ of 40 m =   **d** $\frac{3}{4}$ of 36 litres =

e $\frac{2}{3}$ of 30 =   **f** $\frac{2}{3}$ of 24 =   **g** $\frac{2}{5}$ of 15 kg =

h $\frac{2}{5}$ of £30 =   **i** $\frac{3}{5}$ of £50 =   **j** $\frac{2}{3}$ of 24 mm =

4 James has 25 pens.
He gives his sister $\frac{2}{5}$ of the pens.
How many pens does he give her?

This spread will show you how to:

▶▶ Write fractions as a division.
▶▶ Find simple percentages of quantities.

KEYWORDS

| Percentage | Fraction |
| Reduce | Increase |

▷ A percentage is a fraction out of 100: 40% = $\frac{40}{100}$.

Sale signs often use percentages:

... means you pay
one half ($\frac{1}{2}$) of the price.

SALE 10% OFF

... means take $\frac{1}{10}$th
off the price.

... means reduce the
price by one quarter ($\frac{1}{4}$).

You find a percentage of an amount by finding the fraction:

▶ To find $\frac{1}{10}$ or 10% you divide by 10.
▶ To find $\frac{1}{5}$ or 20% you divide by 5.
▶ To find $\frac{1}{4}$ or 25% you divide by 4.
▶ To find $\frac{1}{2}$ or 50% you divide by 2.

example

Work out how much you save with these sale prices:
a 10% off £50
b 50% off £240

. . . .

a 10% is the same as $\frac{1}{10}$.
$\frac{1}{10}$ of £50 means £50 ÷ 10
50 ÷ 10 = 5
So you save £5.

b 50% is the same as $\frac{1}{2}$.
$\frac{1}{2}$ of £240 means £240 ÷ 2.
240 ÷ 2 is 120.
So you save £120.

You can also increase an amount by a percentage.

I'm going to increase your
pocket money by 20%

The bad news is,
I'm going to start charging
you for food!

Yesssss...
20% is $\frac{2}{10}$ or $\frac{1}{5}$.
My pocket money is £30 a week.
$\frac{1}{5}$ of £30   £30 ÷ 5 = £6
I'll get an extra £6 a week.

Exercise N5.8

1 Estimate the percentage of each shape that is coloured.

a  **b**  **c**   **d**

2 Find 50% of these amounts.

  a £8   **b** £12   **c** £20   **d** £30   **e** £84

3 Find 10% of these amounts.

  a £40   **b** £90   **c** £50   **d** £120   **e** £240

4 a This handbag was £22.

It is reduced by 50%.
How much do you save?

  b This DVD was £20.

It is reduced by 10%.
How much do you save?

  c This tennis racquet was £44.

It is reduced by 25%.
How much do you save?

  d These football boots were £80.

They are reduced by 20%.
How much do you save?

5 Work out:

  a 20% of £30   **b** 20% of £40   **c** 30% of £30
  d 40% of £20   **e** 30% of £50   **f** 60% of £20

6 Liz pays £100 a week rent for her flat.
The rent is increased by 10%.
How much more does she pay each week?

7 Liz earns £340 a week as a receptionist.
Her wages are increased by 10%.
How much more does she get each week?

8 Liz's bus fares are £12.50 each week.
They increase by 50%.
How much more do her bus fares cost each week?

9 Liz goes to the cinema each Saturday night with her friends.
The admission prices go up from £10 by 20%.
How much does a ticket cost now?

You should know how to ...

1 Find all the factor pairs of a number.
  ▶ The factor pairs of 16 are:
  1 and 16, 2 and 8, 4 and 4.

2 Round a number to the nearest whole number.
  ▶ 2.3 is between 2 and 3:

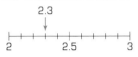

  2.3 is 2 to the nearest whole number.

3 Write fractions as a division.
  ▶ To find $\frac{1}{3}$ you divide by 3.
  $\frac{1}{3}$ of 12 = 12 ÷ 3 = 4

4 Use all four operations to solve word problems.

Check out

1 Find all the factor pairs of 48.

2 Round these amounts to the nearest whole
  kilogram:
  3.2 kg   4.7 kg   14.3 kg
  18.6 kg   6.5 kg   12.2 kg

3 Find:
  a $\frac{1}{2}$ of 700 g
  b $\frac{1}{4}$ of 400 kg
  c $\frac{1}{3}$ of £150
  d $\frac{1}{5}$ of 200 litres
  e $\frac{1}{10}$ of 340 cm
  f $\frac{1}{8}$ of 160 m.

4 **a** There are 12 eggs in a box.
    How many eggs are there in 9 boxes?
    How many boxes do you need for 192 eggs?
  b Josh saved 15p a week for one year.
    How much did he save?

The handling data cycle

This unit will show you how to:

▶▶ Solve a problem by representing and interpreting data in tables, charts and diagrams, including:
  ▶ pictograms
  ▶ bar charts
  ▶ bar line charts
  ▶ line graphs.

▶▶ Find the mode of a set of data.
▶▶ Explain methods and reasoning, orally and in writing.

You can collect data on what people eat at lunchtime in school.

Before you start

You should know how to ...

1 Draw a pictogram and a bar chart to represent data.

Check in

1 This data shows the favourite colours of students in class 7B.

Colour	Blue	Red	Green	Yellow	Orange
Frequency	7	9	6	4	5

a Draw a pictogram to represent this data.

b Draw a bar chart to represent this data.

This spread will show you how to:

▶▶ Solve a problem by collecting and organising data in tally charts and frequency tables.

KEYWORDS

Collect	Results
Tally chart	Count
Frequency table	

Marvin runs the school canteen.
He wants to provide healthy food for everyone to eat.

He asks students to tell him their favourite vegetable.
He collects the results in a tally chart:

Favourite vegetable	Tally	Frequency
Broccoli	⊞⊞ ⊞⊞ ⊞⊞	
Cabbage	⊞⊞	
Carrots	⊞⊞ ⊞⊞ ⊞⊞ ⊞⊞ ⊞⊞ ⊞⊞	
Cauliflower	⊞⊞ ⊞⊞	
Peas	⊞⊞ ⊞⊞ ⊞⊞ ⊞⊞ ⊞⊞	
Spinach	⊞⊞ ⊞⊞	
Sweetcorn	⊞⊞ ⊞⊞ ⊞⊞ ⊞⊞	

He limits the options to vegetables he knows are available at a reasonable price all year round.

He collects the results in groups of five so they are easier to read.

⊞⊞ ⊞⊞ ⊞⊞ ⊞⊞ ⊞⊞ means 25 votes.

He will count up the tallies and put the totals in a frequency column.

▶ You can collect data in a tally chart.

▶ You count up the tallies to make a frequency table.

You may want to limit the options that people can choose from
to make the data more useful.

Exercise D3.3

1 The table shows the favourite teams of class 7F.

Team	City	United	Town	Rovers
Frequency	12	4	8	6

Draw a bar chart to display this data.

2 The table shows the number of children in students' families.

Number of children	0	1	2	3	4
Frequency	4	16	14	4	1

Copy and complete the bar line graph to display this data.

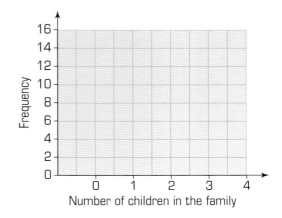

3 Draw a bar chart to display this data:

Flower	Rose	Crocus	Daisy	Tulip	Primrose
Number found in the garden	10	20	25	15	5

Choose an appropriate scale to use on the axis.
Remember to label each axis and give your chart a title.

4 The table shows the number of people on a local bus at different times one Monday.

Time	0800	0820	0840	0900	0920
People on the bus	35	40	45	25	10

Copy and complete the line graph to display this data.

Plot the points, then join them with a straight line.

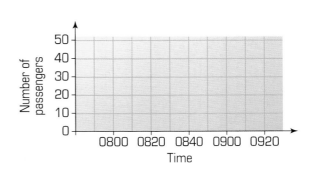

This spread will show you how to:

▶▶ Interpret data in tables and charts.
▶▶ Find the mode of a set of data.

KEYWORDS
Highest   Frequency
Data   Mode

Marvin can see that carrots are the most popular vegetable from the bar chart.

It has the highest bar so it is the most common answer.

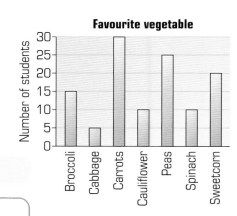

Favourite vegetable

▶ The most common item in a set of data is the mode.

example

Find the mode of this set of data:

| red | red | blue | green |
| blue | red | yellow | green |

....

Red is the most common colour in this list.
The mode is red.

This data has two modes: 2 and 4.

② ② 1 ④ 3 ④

They both appear twice. The others appear only once.

You can find the mode from a frequency table.

example

Find the mode of this set of data.

Score on a dice	Frequency
1	6
2	4
3	5
4	6
5	8
6	7

The most common score is 5. It appears 8 times.

The mode is 5.

▶ The mode is the item with the highest frequency.

Exercise D3.4

1 The pictogram shows the CDs bought by class 7E last summer.

Which was the most popular CD?
This is the mode.

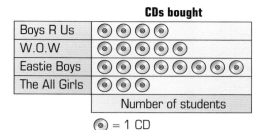

CDs bought

Boys R Us	◎ ◎ ◎ ◎
W.O.W	◎ ◎ ◎ ◎ ◎
Eastie Boys	◎ ◎ ◎ ◎ ◎ ◎ ◎ ◎
The All Girls	◎ ◎ ◎

Number of students

◎ = 1 CD

2 The bar line graph shows the number of CDs sold by a group each month.

In which month did they sell most copies?
This is the mode.

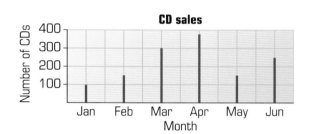

3 The data shows how some students travel to school.

Car	Bike	Bus	Bus
Walk	Train	Car	Car
Train	Walk	Walk	Bike
Walk	Bus	Bike	Walk

What is the most common method of travel?
This is the mode.

4 The data shows the marks scored out of 10 in a test.

4   6   8   10   9   6   7   3   8   6

What is the mode of this data?

5 The table shows the types of jobs students do at home.

What is the most common job for students to do?
This is the mode.

Job	Frequency
Hoovering	7
Gardening	3
Cooking	12
Washing up	9
Washing the car	5

6 Challenge
Write down a list of colours so that red is the mode.

This spread will show you how to:

▶▶ Interpret data in tables, charts, graphs and diagrams.

KEYWORDS
Interpret   Bar chart
Diagram

Marvin presents his results to the governors.

He suggests his results show he should offer the same three vegetables every day:

Carrots (30 votes)   Peas (25 votes)   and   Sweetcorn (20 votes)

The governors agree but also want him to offer broccoli (15 votes).

You should always interpret your diagrams.

example

The bar chart shows the after school activities of students at Sports Academy.

a Which activity is the most popular?

b The Academy needs to cut costs. Which activity should they drop and why?

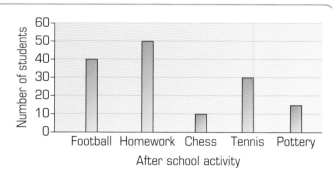

a Homework club is the most popular.

b Chess is the least popular but it doesn't cost much money to run. They could decide to drop pottery as it is more expensive.

Exercise D3.5

1 The chart shows the results of a survey
into preferred yoghurt flavours.
Which was the most popular flavour?
Which two flavours got the same
number of votes?

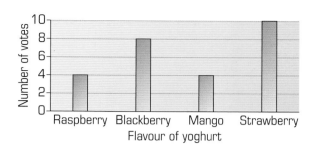

2 These charts show some data for a new pop
band called The Frames.
   a In which month did they sell the most CDs?
      Why do you think this was?
   b How many CDs did they sell in December?
   c In which month did most people buy
      their CD?
   d Why do you think there were no CD sales
      in November?

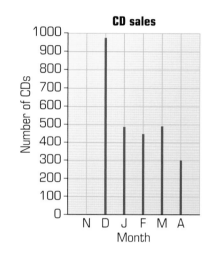

3 These three diagrams show information about
fruit gums.

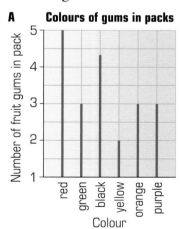

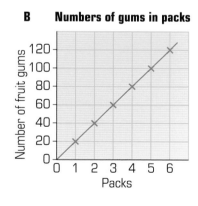

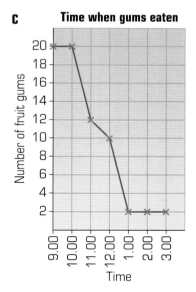

Use the graphs to answer these questions.
Write which graph you use, A, B or C.
The first one is done for you.
   a How many fruit gums in two packs?   Answer: Graph B. 40 fruit gums.
   b How many yellows in a pack?   c How many fruit gums in four packs?
   d How many were left at midday?   e How many green and orange in one pack?

You should know how to ...

1 Represent data in frequency tables.

Check out

1 Copy and complete this frequency table showing the scores on a dice rolled 50 times

Score	Tally	Frequency
1	JHT IIII	
2		10
3	JHT III	
4		6
5	JHT IIII	
6	JHT III	

2 Represent data in bar line graphs.
> A bar line graph uses lines to represent data.

2 Draw the data from question 1 on a bar line graph.
Copy this grid to start you off.

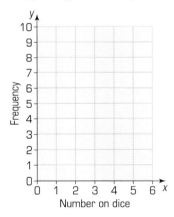

3 Find the mode of a set of data.
> The mode is the most common item in a set of data.

3 What is the model score on the dice in question 1?
How can you tell?

Probability experiments

This unit will show you how to:

▶▶ Discuss the chance or likelihood of particular events.

▶▶ Collect, organise and interpret data in tables.

▶▶ Discuss the difference between theory and actual results.

You can use probability to work out your chance of winning.

Before you start

You should know how to ...

1 Recognise odd and even numbers.

2 Use fraction notation.
  ▶ You write 3 out of 4 as $\frac{3}{4}$.

Check in

1 Which of these numbers are even?

  5 23 16 8 20 61

2 Write these amounts using fraction notation:
  a 3 out of 5
  b 1 out of 6
  c 2 out of 3.

This spread will show you how to:

▶▶ Discuss the chance or likelihood of particular events.

Gemma and Liam are playing 'Snakes and Ladders'.

The first person to roll a 6 with a dice starts.

There are six possible outcomes when you roll a dice:

One outcome is a 6.

The probability of rolling a 6 is one chance in six, or $\frac{1}{6}$.

▶ Probability is a measure of likelihood.

You can place probabilities on a probability scale:

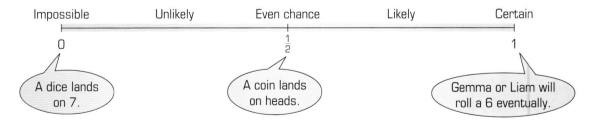

The probability of rolling a 6 with a dice is $\frac{1}{6}$ – it is unlikely:

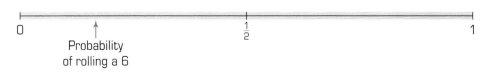

Exercise D4.1

1 Match each of these words to the events listed.

Impossible   Unlikely   Likely   Certain

a You will watch television tonight.   **b** It will snow next August.
c You will grow taller than your teacher.   **d** It will get dark tonight.
e It will rain tomorrow.

2 Copy this scale and mark on each of the events in question 1.

No chance   Poor chance   Even chance   Good chance   Certain

3 Copy and complete these statements to find the probability of each event.
The first one is done for you.

a A dice will land on a 4.

> There are six possible outcomes.
> One of the outcomes is a 4.
> There is a one in six chance of rolling a 4.
> The probability of rolling a 4 is $\frac{1}{6}$.

b A dice will land on a 5.

> There are ___ possible outcomes.
> ___ of the outcomes is a 5.
> There is a ___ in ___ chance of rolling a 5.
> The probability of rolling a 5 is ___.

c A dice will land on an even number.

The even numbers are 2, 4, 6, 8, 10 …

> There are ___ possible outcomes.
> ___ of the outcomes is an even number.
> There is a ___ in ___ chance of rolling an even number.
> The probability of rolling an even number is ___ .

4 List the possible outcomes when you:
a Flip a coin
b Choose a number between 1 and 10
c Choose a letter from the word CERTAIN.

This spread will show you how to:

▶▶ Discuss the chance or likelihood of particular events.
▶▶ Collect, organise and interpret data in tables.

KEYWORDS

Chance
Probability
Fraction
Frequency table
Tally
Outcome
Frequent
Experiment

Gemma and Liam are discussing 'Snakes and Ladders'.

6 has the best chance of coming up!

All the numbers have an equal chance.

They roll a dice 50 times to see who is correct.
They record their results in a frequency table.

Dice score	Tally	Frequency (total)
1	卌 l	6
2	llll	4
3	卌 卌 ll	12
4	卌 llll	9
5	卌 卌 l	11
6	卌 lll	8

example

Use the data from the table to answer these questions.

a What is the most frequent score on the dice?
b What is the least frequent score?
c Do these results show that Liam was correct?
d What is the probability of scoring 6 with one throw?

....

a The most frequent score is 3.
b The least frequent score is 2.
c No, 3 has the best chance of coming up.
d As a fraction, the chance of getting a 6 is $\frac{8}{50}$.

Exercise D4.2

1 Copy and complete this statement to find the probability
of getting a 4 from the table on page 212:

> There are 50 outcomes.
> ___ outcomes are a 4.
> The chance of getting a 4 is ___ out of 50.
> As a fraction, the probability of getting a 4 is $\frac{}{50}$.

2 Use the table and follow the working in question 1.
Write down the probability of each of these scores as a fraction.
   a 3   **b** 2   **c** 1   **d** 5

3 **a** Carry out the experiment shown on page 212.

   ▸ Roll a dice 50 times.
   ▸ Keep a tally of results in this table:

   b Are your results the same or different to
   Gemma and Liam's?
   c Do your results suggest that 6 has the best
   chance of coming up?

Score on dice	Tally	Frequency
1		
2		
3		
4		
5		
6		

4 **Coin experiment**
When you flip a coin it can land in two ways.

It can land on 'heads'   or it can land on 'tails'.

Outcome	Tally	Frequency (total)
Heads		
Tails		

   a Copy this frequency table.
   b Flip a coin 50 times and record your results as a tally.
   c Which was the most frequent outcome?

This spread will show you how to:
▶▶ Discuss the difference between theory and actual results.

KEYWORDS
Outcome   Result
Probability   Trial
Experiment

When you flip a coin there are two possible outcomes:

    heads   or   tails.

There are two outcomes.
One outcome is tails.
The probability of getting a tail is 1 in 2 or $\frac{1}{2}$.

Paul and Hacibe test a 1 euro coin.

They flip the coin 20 times and record the results:

Outcome	Tally	Frequency
Heads	ЖЖ ЖЖ II	12
Tails	ЖЖ III	8

Each result is called a trial.

They discuss their results:

Hacibe says: *There are more heads than tails – they should be the same.*

Paul says: *They are nearly the same, though!*

They decide to experiment further.
They flip the coin 100 times:

They carry out more trials.

Outcome	Tally	Frequency
Heads	ЖЖ ЖЖ ЖЖ ЖЖ ЖЖ ЖЖ ЖЖ ЖЖ ЖЖ I	46
Tails	ЖЖ ЖЖ ЖЖ ЖЖ ЖЖ ЖЖ ЖЖ ЖЖ ЖЖ ЖЖ IIII	54

The numbers of heads and tails are quite close.
Paul and Hacibe think if they do more trials the
probabilities will get even closer to $\frac{1}{2}$.

Exercise D4.3

1 For these results:

  a Write down the total number of trials.

  b Write down the number of heads.

  c Write down the probability of getting a head.

  d Which result is more likely: heads or tails?

  e Mark the probability of getting heads on a copy of this scale:

Outcome	Frequency
Heads	12
Tails	8

```
├────────┼────────┼────────┼────────┤
impossible   unlikely   even chance   likely   certain
```

2 For these results:

  a How many trials are there altogether?

  b Which result is more likely: heads or tails?

  c Copy this probability scale:

Outcome	Frequency
Heads	46
Tails	54

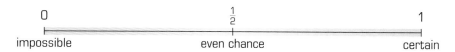

```
0                    ½                    1
├────────────────────┼────────────────────┤
impossible        even chance         certain
```

   Mark the probability of getting each outcome on your scale.

3 Take two coins and stick them together using sticky tape.
Make sure that two different faces are showing:

  heads   and   tails.

  a Which outcome do you think is most likely when you drop the coins, or are they equally likely?

  b Copy this frequency table.

Outcome	Tally	Frequency (total)
Heads		
Tails		

  c Drop the coins 50 times and record your results as a tally.
Total your results.
Was your guess correct?

You should know how to …

1 Discuss the chance or likelihood of particular events.

Check out

1 Write these events in order of likelihood

   A I will meet an alien tonight.

   B I will drink some milk tomorrow.

   C I will eat later today.

   D It will snow this year.

   E The leaves will fall off some trees next Autumn.

Mark the events on a copy of this scale:

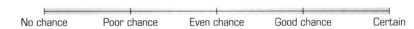

No chance   Poor chance   Even chance   Good chance   Certain

2 Represent and interpret data in tables.

2 This table shows the results of a survey into pets owned by class 7B.

Number of pets	Tally	Frequency
0	III	3
1	JHT JHT I	11
2	IIII	4
3	JHT II	7
4	III	3
5	II	2

   a How many students have no pets?

   b What is the most common number of pets?

   c How many students had more than three pets?

   d How many students took part in the survey?

5 Equations and graphs

This unit will show you how to:

▶▶ Understand the links between the four operations.

▶▶ Use known facts and place value to multiply mentally.

▶▶ Explain a formula in words.

▶▶ Recognise and extend number sequences.

▶▶ Plot coordinates in the first quadrant.

▶▶ Write a formula using symbols.

▶▶ Plot points in all four quadrants.

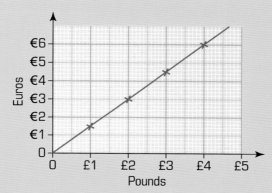

You can use this graph to change pounds into euros.

Before you start

You should know how to ...

1 Recognise and order negative numbers.

2 Plot points on a coordinate grid.

Check in

1 a Which of these temperatures are below 0°C?

5°C   1°C   ⁻3°C   ⁻12°C

b Order the temperatures, starting with the coldest.

2 Copy this grid:

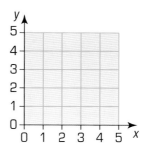

Plot the points

(1, 2)   (2, 3)   (4, 5)

Join them. What do you notice?

This spread will show you how to:

▶▶ Understand the links between the four operations.

KEYWORDS
Equation   Inverse

You can write this puzzle as an equation.

You can use x to represent the starting number.

The equation is $x + 8 = 13$

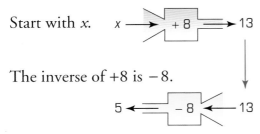

starting number   add 8   you get 13

> What is my mystery number?
> I start with a number.
> I add 8 to it and I get 13.
> What was the number that I
> started with?

To find the value of x you can work backwards.

  ▶ **To work backwards you use the inverse.**

Start with x. $x \longrightarrow \boxed{+8} \longrightarrow 13$

The inverse of $+8$ is -8.

$5 \longleftarrow \boxed{-8} \longleftarrow 13$

$13 - 8 = 5$, so the starting number must be 5.

  ▶ **The inverse of adding is subtracting.**

You can use inverses in multiplication or division problems.

  ▶ **The inverse of multiplying is dividing.**

example

a
> I think of a number. I multiply the number
> by 5 and I get 50.
> What was the number that I started with?

b
> I think of a number and I divide it by 2,
> now I have 6. What number did I start with?

a Start with x. $x \longrightarrow \boxed{\times 5} \longrightarrow 50$

The inverse of $\times 5$ is $\div 5$.

$10 \longleftarrow \boxed{\div 5} \longleftarrow 50$

$50 \div 5 = 10$ so $x = 10$
(you began with 10)

b Start with t. $t \longrightarrow \boxed{\div 2} \longrightarrow 6$

The inverse of $\div 2$ is $\times 2$.

$12 \longleftarrow \boxed{\times 2} \longleftarrow 6$

$6 \times 2 = 12$, so $t = 12$
(you began with 12)

Exercise A5.1

1 Find the starting numbers in each of these puzzles.
You can probably do most of them in your head.
  a I think of a number. I add 3. Now I have 10.
  b I think of a number and add 20. Now I have 30.
  c I think of a number and subtract 6. Now I have 5.
  d I think of a number and multiply it by 4. Now I have 8.
  e I think of a number and divide it by 3. Now I have 10.
  f I think of a number. I divide it by 5. Now I have 20.
  g I think of a number. I multiply it by 6. Now I have 18.

2 Find the value of x using the inverse diagram:
$x + 25 = 34$

Start with x: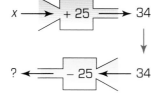

3 Make a diagram for this equation: $n - 12 = 21$.
  a Start by copying a diagram like this one.

Start with n: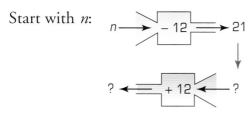

  b Fill in the blank spaces.
  c Find the value of n.

4 Use the inverse to find the values of these symbols.
Use a drawing to help you think about the right steps to take.
  a $x + 10 = 19$ **b** $c + 7 = 19$ **c** $b + 5 = 18$
  d $f - 5 = 10$ **e** $h - 3 = 8$ **f** $j - 7 = 3$
  g $4 \times d = 20$ **h** $5 \times t = 50$ **i** $m \times 3 = 12$
  j $k \div 2 = 10$ **k** $y \times 4 = 12$ **l** $g \div 5 = 2$

> The multiplication table on page 118 will help you with the multiplication and division problems.

This spread will show you how to:

▶▶ Use known facts and place value to multiply mentally.
▶▶ Explain a formula in words.

KEYWORDS
Formula   Wage
Multiply

Mike works in a factory making cars.
He is paid £30 for every car he makes.

If he makes 2 cars, he is paid 2 × £30 = £60.
If he makes 6 cars, he is paid 6 × £30 = £180.

To calculate Mike's wage, you multiply £30 by the
number of cars that he makes.

You can use a formula to calculate his wage:

▶ **Wage = £30 × number of cars made**

You can use this formula to work out Mike's wage.

---

example

How much does Mike earn if he makes:

a   4 cars   **b**   9 cars?

....

a   If Mike makes 4 cars, the formula is:
     Wage = £30 × 4
           = £120

b   If Mike makes 9 cars, the formula is:
     Wage = £30 × 9
           = £270

30 = 10 × 3
To multiply by 30:
▶ multiply by 10 then
▶ multiply by 3.

    30 × 4 = 4 × 10 × 3
            = 40 × 3
            = 120

Exercise A5.2

1 Use Mike's wage formula to work out his wages when he makes these numbers of cars. The formula is:

> ▶ Wage = £30 × number of cars he makes

Use the £ sign in your answers.

a 1 car   **b** 5 cars   **c** 8 cars   **d** 9 cars
e 10 cars   **f** 12 cars   **g** 14 cars   **h** 0 cars.

2 The formula for wages is changed and Mike gets more money. The new formula is:

> ▶ Wage = £40 × number of cars he makes

Work out Mike's wages using this formula when he makes these numbers of cars.
Use the £ sign in your answers.

a 2 cars   **b** 3 cars   **c** 5 cars   **d** 8 cars
e 4 cars   **f** 7 cars   **g** 1 car   **h** 10 cars.

> Think of £40 as 4 × £10.

3 Lizzie delivers parcels.
She is paid 50p for every parcel that she delivers.
Copy and complete Lizzie's wage formula:

> ▶ Wage = 50p × _____

4 Use the formula you found in question 3 to calculate Lizzie's wages when she delivers:

a 1 parcel   **b** 2 parcels   **c** 4 parcels
d 3 parcels   **e** 10 parcels   **f** 12 parcels
g 20 parcels   **h** 7 parcels   **i** 11 parcels.

5 Pham makes electronic games.
He is paid £50 for every game that he makes.
Write a formula to calculate the money that he is paid.

This spread will show you how to:

▶▶ Explain a formula in words.

KEYWORDS
Symbol   Pattern
Mapping   Formula

A pattern connects the number of shirts on the line and the number of pegs used to hang them.

You can show the pattern as a mapping:

```
shirts  ───────▶  pegs
  1    ───────▶    2    = 1 + 1
  2    ───────▶    3    = 2 + 1
  3    ───────▶    4    = 3 + 1
```

You can write the mapping as a formula:

▶ **The number of pegs = the number of shirts + 1**

For 7 shirts you will need:
7 + 1 pegs = 8 pegs

You can write the formula using symbols as shorthand.
Use s for the number of shirts, and p for the number of pegs.

The formula is: $p = s + 1$

For 6 shirts, $s = 6$ so $p = 6 + 1$

$$p = 7$$

You would need 7 pegs.

example

Ronan has 5 pegs.
How many shirts can he hang?

....

Use the formula: $p = s + 1$
There are 5 pegs, so $p = 5$.

$5 = s + 1$
$5 = 4 + 1$ so $s = 4$.
There will be 4 shirts on the line.

Use the inverse:

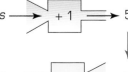

Exercise A5.3

1 Calculate the number of pegs you need to hang these numbers of shirts.

> ▶ $p = s + 1$ where s is the number of shirts, and p is the number of pegs.

The first one is done for you.
a 12 shirts. $p = 12 + 1$ so $p = 13$. You need 13 pegs.

b 25 shirts   **c** 19 shirts   **d** 34 shirts   **e** 99 shirts

2 Use the formula in question 1 to calculate the number of shirts that you can hang with these numbers of pegs.
The first one is done for you.
a 8 pegs $8 = s + 1$ so $s = 7$. You can hang 7 shirts.

b 11 pegs   **c** 4 pegs   **d** 15 pegs   **e** 20 pegs
f 31 pegs   **g** 51 pegs   **h** 25 pegs   **i** 32 pegs.

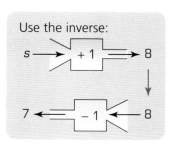

Use the inverse:

3 Use this new formula to calculate the values of p.

> ▶ $p = s + 3$

The first one has been done for you.
a $p = s + 3$ and $s = 4$
$p = 4 + 3$ so $p = 7$

b $p = s + 3$ and $s = 6$ **c** $p = s + 3$ and $s = 9$
d $p = s + 3$ and $s = 12$ **e** $p = s + 3$ and $s = 17$

4 a Count the number of triangles and matches in each drawing of this pattern.

1 triangle   ? triangles
3 matches   ? matches

b Copy and complete this mapping

number of triangles		number of matches
1	⟶	3 = (1 + 2)
2	⟶	? = (2 + ?)
3	⟶	? = (3 + ?)
4	⟶	? = (4 + ?)

c Copy and complete this formula:

> ▶ Number of matches = number of triangles + _____

d Write the formula using symbols.
Use t for the number of triangles and m for the number of matches.

This spread will show you how to:

▶▶ Recognise and extend number sequences.

KEYWORDS
Rule   Increase
Sequence   Pattern

Leaves grow on this stem in a pattern.

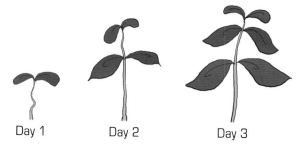

Day 1   Day 2   Day 3

You can write the pattern as a sequence:

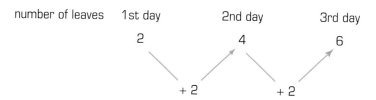

number of leaves   1st day   2nd day   3rd day
                         2   4   6

                              + 2   + 2

The number of leaves increases each day.

Each day the plant grows 2 more leaves.
The rule is: + 2

You can use the rule to calculate how many leaves there will be on the stem on a given day.

example

a Find the number of leaves on the 4th day.
b Find the number of leaves on the 5th day.
c The 10th day pattern in the sequence has 20 leaves.
   How many leaves does the 21st pattern have?

....

a The 4th day pattern has 6 + 2 = 8 leaves.
b The 5th day pattern has 8 + 2 = 10 leaves.
c The 21st pattern has 20 + 2 = 22 leaves.

Exercise A5.4

1 In this café, each table has 3 chairs.

   a Write the first three table patterns as a sequence.
Use these headings:

   Number of tables   **Number of chairs**

   b Copy and complete this rule:

> The rule to move from one pattern to the next
> in the sequence is:

2 Continue the sequence in question 1 until you know how
many chairs are in the 7th pattern.

3 This pattern is made from matchsticks:

   a Write down the number of matchsticks in each pattern.
   b How do you move from one pattern to the next?
Write this as a sentence.

> To move from one pattern to the next you _____.

   c How many matches will there be in the 4th pattern?
   d How many matches will there be in the 5th pattern?
   e Which pattern is made from 16 matches?

4 These are the 3rd and 4th patterns in a matchstick pattern:
Copy and complete this sequence for the pattern.

```
  __      __      7       9       __
    \    /  \    /  \    /  \    /
     +2      +2      +2      +2
```

This spread will show you how to:

▶▶ Recognise and extend number sequences.

KEYWORDS
Pattern   Mapping
Diagram   Rule
Calculation

The number of chairs grows with the number of tables in this pattern.

You can write the pattern as a mapping:

tables	⟶	chairs
2	⟶	6
3	⟶	9
4	⟶	12

There are 3 chairs for every one table.
There are 3 times the number of chairs as tables.

The rule that connects the number of tables and chairs is:

You can use the rule to calculate the number of chairs needed for the number of tables.

If you have 5 tables you will need:

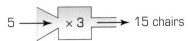

5 ⟶ × 3 ⟶ 15 chairs

This diagram shows four different calculations:

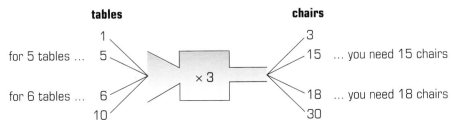

	tables		chairs	
	1		3	
for 5 tables …	5	× 3	15	… you need 15 chairs
for 6 tables …	6		18	… you need 18 chairs
	10		30	

Exercise A5.5

1 Copy and complete these diagrams.
They show the number of chairs needed for the number
of tables using different rules.

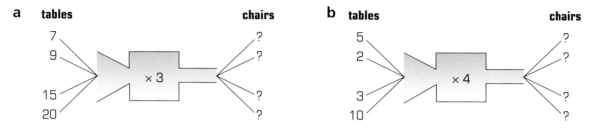

2 This necklace is made from blue and red beads.

a Use the bead pattern to copy and complete this mapping.

blue		red
1	⟶	?
2	⟶	?
3	⟶	?

b Work out the rule that connects the blue and red beads.
c Use this rule to extend the mapping:

blue		red
10	⟶	?
30	⟶	?
50	⟶	?
45	⟶	?

3 Here are some mappings for blue and red beads.
Find the rule for each mapping.

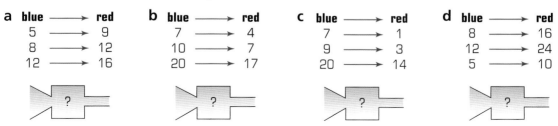

This spread will show you how to:
▶▶ Plot coordinates in the first quadrant.
▶▶ Recognise and extend number sequences.

KEYWORDS
Coordinates   Mapping
Pattern   Rule

This necklace has a pattern of red and blue beads.

You can show the pattern on a graph.
First write the pattern as a mapping:

blue ⟶ **red**
1 ⟶ 2
2 ⟶ 4
3 ⟶ 6

The rule is 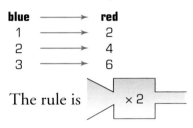 × 2

You plot the pairs of values as coordinates:
(1, 2)   (2, 4)   (3, 6).

You can extend the line to find other pairs of
red and blue beads.

The dotted line continues the same rule
between the red and blue beads.

The coordinates (4, 8) (5, 10) (6, 12) are also
on the line.

These values follow the same rule:

blue ⟶ **red**
4 ⟶ 8
5 ⟶ 10
6 ⟶ 12

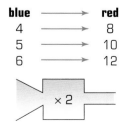 × 2

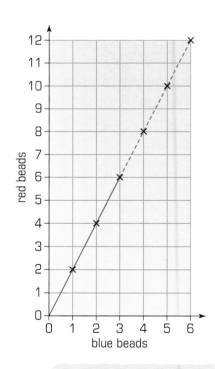

Any pairs of coordinates that
follow the rule will also be on
the line.

Exercise A5.6

1 Here is a pattern of green and yellow beads.

  a Copy and complete the mapping to show the connection between the number of green and yellow beads

```
green  ──────▶  yellow
  1    ──────▶    1
  2    ──────▶    ?
  3    ──────▶    3
  4    ──────▶    ?
  5    ──────▶    5
```

  b Write the values on the mapping as coordinates: (1, 1) …

  c Draw a grid from 0 to 10 in both directions.

  d Plot your coordinates onto the grid.

  e Join the points with a straight line.

  f Extend the line at both ends.

  g What is the rule that connects the number of green and yellow beads?

  h If the necklace has 8 green beads, how many yellow beads will it need?

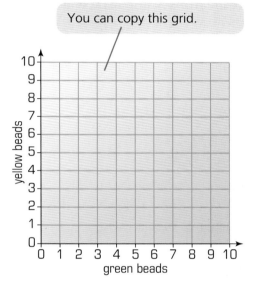

You can copy this grid.

2 The graph shows the connection between white and black beads.

  a Write the coordinates of the three points shown on the line.

  b Copy and complete this mapping to show the three coordinates:

```
white  ──────▶  black
  1    ──────▶    ?
  2    ──────▶    ?
  3    ──────▶    ?
```

  c What is the rule that connects the number of white and black beads?

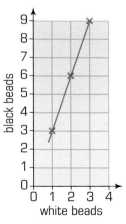

3 Imagine the line is extended in question 2.
Copy and complete these coordinates to show a point on the line: (4, ?)

This spread will show you how to:

▶▶ Plot coordinates in the first quadrant.
▶▶ Write a formula using symbols.

KEYWORDS
Formula   Graph
Mapping
Coordinates
Straight line

Angela irons shirts.
She is paid £4 an hour and £1 for each shirt she irons.

If she irons 3 shirts she will be paid 3 × £1 plus £4.

You can write this as a formula.
Use n for the number of shirts ironed.
Use w for Angela's wage.

The formula is:

▶ $w = n + 4$

You write $n \times 1$ as n.

You can draw a graph for this formula and use it to calculate Angela's wages.

You use the formula to calculate the coordinates for the graph.

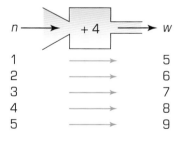

n →	+ 4	→ w
1	→	5
2	→	6
3	→	7
4	→	8
5	→	9

The points are in a straight line.

You can extend the line to find Angela's wages without having to calculate.

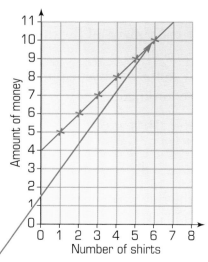

Angela would earn £10
if she ironed 6 shirts.

Exercise A5.7

1 Use the graph on page 230 to say how much Angela will earn when she irons 7 shirts.

2 The formula for Pete's wage is: $w = n + 2$.
   a Copy and complete the mapping diagram for Pete's wages.

You can copy this grid.

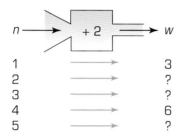

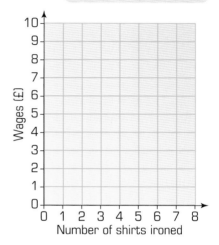

   b Plot the pairs of coordinates onto a grid.
   c Use an arrow to point to Pete's wage when he irons 7 shirts.
   d How much would Pete be paid for ironing 8 shirts? Show this point on your graph.

3 Beverly is paid £2 per shirt.
   The formula for Beverley's wage is: $w = 2 \times n$.
   a Copy and complete this mapping for Beverley's wage formula.

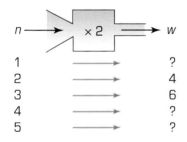

   b Draw another pair of axes.
   c Extend the vertical axis up to £20.
   d Plot the pairs of coordinates onto the graph.
   e Check that the points on the graph make a straight line and join them by drawing the line.
   f Use arrows to show Beverley's wage when she irons:
      i   7 shirts
      ii 9 shirts
      iii 10 shirts.

This spread will show you how to:

▶▶ Plot points in all four quadrants.

KEYWORDS
Quadrant   Axes
Coordinates   Negative

On a number line:
▶ Positive numbers are to the right of 0.
▶ Negative numbers are to the left of 0.

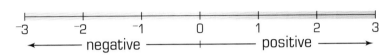

Coordinate axes extend to include negative numbers.

The grid is divided into four sections.
Each section is called a quadrant.

Second quadrant
B is (⁻4, 3)

4 left   3 up

First quadrant
A is (2, 6)

2 right   6 up

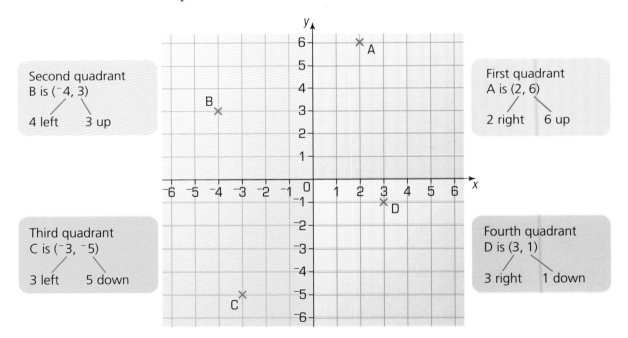

Third quadrant
C is (⁻3, ⁻5)

3 left   5 down

Fourth quadrant
D is (3, 1)

3 right   1 down

▶ On a coordinate grid:
  ▶ You move along the *x*-axis first.
    You move left or right (horizontally).
  ▶ You move along the *y*-axis second.
    You move up or down (vertically).

Right is positive (+).   Left is negative (–).

Up is positive (+).   Down is negative (–).

Exercise A5.8

1 These coordinates will lead you to the letters on the grid that will make a tongue-twister.

Spell the words one at a time until you finish the sentence.

This is the first word.
(1, 4)   (⁻1, 1)   (⁻2, 3)
  T   H   E

(1, 4) (⁻1, 1) (⁻2, 3)

(4, 1) (2, ⁻3) (⁻5, ⁻4)

(⁻3, ⁻2) (2, 3) (4, ⁻1) (⁻4, 4)

(⁻3, ⁻2) (4, 4) (4, ⁻4) (⁻4, 2) (⁻2, 3) (1, ⁻1)

(4, 1) (⁻5, ⁻1) (5, ⁻3) (⁻4, 2)

(4, 1) (⁻5, 5) (2, 3) (⁻4, 2) (⁻2, 3)

(⁻3, ⁻2) (4, ⁻1) (4, ⁻4) (1, 2) (⁻2, ⁻4)

(⁻2, 5) (1, ⁻3) (4, ⁻4) (⁻4, 2) (⁻2, 3)

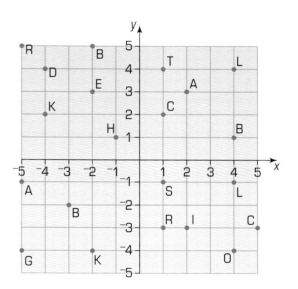

2 a Draw three grids like this one.
  b Plot one of these sets of points on each grid.
  c As you plot each point, join it to the last one.
  d Write the name of each shape that you have drawn.

Set 1: (5, 3) (⁻5, 1) (2, ⁻4) (5, 3)

Set 2: (3, 2) (2, 3) (⁻4, ⁻2) (⁻3, ⁻3) (3, 2)

Set 3: (⁻2, 5) (⁻5, 3) (⁻2, ⁻4) (1, 3) (⁻2, 5)

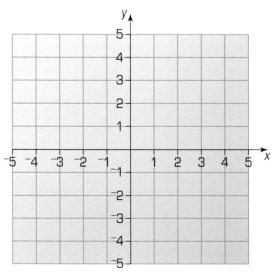

3 In which quadrant do these coordinates belong?
Write: first, second, third or fourth.
  a (⁻3, 5)   **b** (⁻5, ⁻6)   **c** (3, 6)   **d** (6, ⁻8)

You should know how to ...

1 Explain a formula in words.

2 Recognise and extend number sequences.

3 Plot coordinates in the first quadrant.

Check out

1 Explain in words the rule for this sequence:

1, 4, 9, 16, 25, ...

2 Copy and complete these sequences:

a 23, 34, __, __, 67

b __, __, 41, 33, __, 17

3 Plot these coordinates on a copy of this grid:

(1, 4)   (2, 5)   (3, 6)

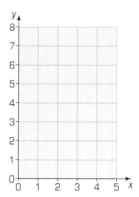

Join the points with a straight line.
Write the coordinates of another point on the line.

Exercise S5.2

1 What type of triangle is each of these shapes?
Choose the answer from the box.

> equilateral   isosceles   right-angled   scalene

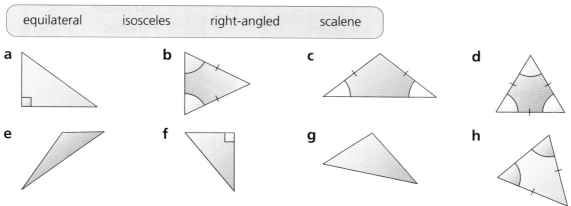

2 Give a reason for each of your answers in question 1.
The first one is done for you.
a It is right-angled because one angle is 90°.

3 What type of triangle is each of these shapes?
Give reasons for your answers.
The first one is done for you.
a It is right-angled.
One of the angles is 90°.

b 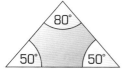   **c**   **d**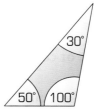

4 What type of quadrilateral is each of these shapes?
a 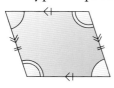   **b**    **c**   **d**

5 A part of each shape is hidden. What could the completed shape be?
a   **b**   **c**   **d**

239

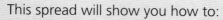

This spread will show you how to:

⏩ Recognise reflective symmetry in regular shapes.

KEYWORDS
Triangle
Half, halves
Line symmetry
Shape
Symmetrical
Regular
Equal sides
Equal angles

You can fold this triangle ...   so the two halves fit together.

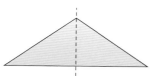

The shape is symmetrical.
The fold line is a line of symmetry.

▶ A shape has line symmetry if you can fold it so that one half fits exactly on top of the other.

You can check using a mirror.

example

Does this triangle have line symmetry?

You cannot fold the triangle into exactly two halves.

It does not have line symmetry.

▶ A regular shape has equal sides and equal angles.

Equilateral triangle   Square   Regular pentagon   Regular hexagon

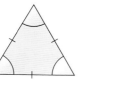

An equilateral triangle has:

3 equal sides
3 equal angles
3 lines of symmetry

A square has:

4 equal sides
4 equal angles
4 lines of symmetry

Exercise S5.4

1 Which of these shapes have line symmetry?

a
b
c
d

2 Copy these shapes onto squared paper and draw any lines of symmetry.

a
b
c
d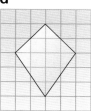
e

3 How many lines of symmetry does each of these shapes have?

a
b
c

d
e
f

4 Find all the lines of symmetry of a regular pentagon.

Copy and complete:
A regular pentagon has:
5 equal sides
5 equal angles
__ lines of symmetry.

5 Find all the lines of symmetry of a regular hexagon.

Copy and complete:
A regular hexagon has:
__ equal sides
__ equal angles
__ lines of symmetry.

This spread will show you how to:

▶▶ Recognise where a shape will be after a rotation.

KEYWORDS

Rotation   Full turn
Turn   Position
Rotational symmetry

The blades of a helicopter rotate:

  ▶ A rotation is a turn.

The position of the blades repeats twice in one full turn:

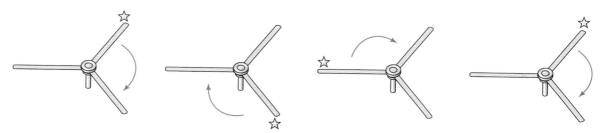

When you rotate this letter through a full turn ...   it only repeats itself at the end.

The letter does not have rotational symmetry.

  ▶ A shape has rotational symmetry if it repeats in a full turn.

You can turn the page to check for rotational symmetry:

This word has rotational symmetry.

 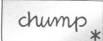  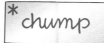

The * helps show when you get back to the start.

Exercise S5.5

1 Which three of these letters have rotational symmetry?
Answer Yes or No.

a **b**  **c** **d** **e**

2 Which of these playing cards have rotational symmetry?

a **b** 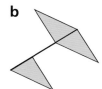 **c** **d** **e**

3 Which of these words have rotational symmetry?
Answer Yes or No. Turn the page to help you decide.

a pod   **b** NOON   **c** dip   **d** MUM   **e** suns

4 Find two more words with rotational symmetry.

5 Which of these shapes have rotational symmetry?

a **b** 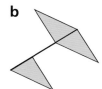 **c** **d**

e **f** **g** **h**

6 The number 1961 has rotational symmetry.
   a Find three more numbers with rotational symmetry.
   b What is the next year that will have rotational symmetry?

This spread will show you how to:

▶▶ Recognise where a shape will be after a translation.

KEYWORDS
Grid   Tessellate
Translation Reflect

You can slide a shape across a grid to a new position:

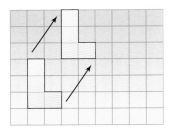

The sliding movement is called a translation.

▶ In a translation you move the shape across first and then up or down.

Copies of this L shape fit together exactly.

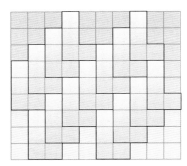

▶ Shapes that tessellate fit together with no gaps or overlaps.

Here are some more examples:

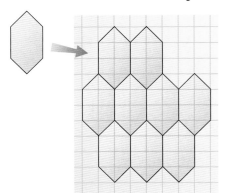

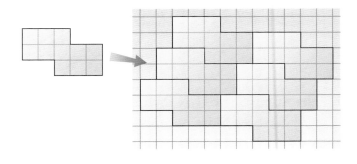

Exercise S5.6

1 Draw these shapes on squared paper.
Use translations to make a tessellation.

a 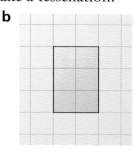 b c 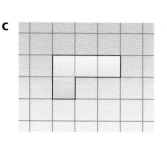 d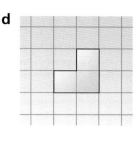

2 You can reflect shapes to tessellate them:

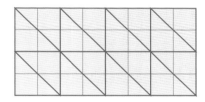

Make ten copies of each shape.
Fit the copies together to show how each shape tessellates.
Draw your results on squared paper.

a  b 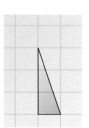 c 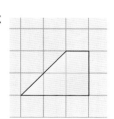 d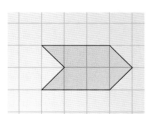

3 Make 12 copies of this L shape.
See if you can tessellate them to make this rectangle.

You should know how to ...

1 Recognise rectangles.

▶ A rectangle has opposite sides equal and parallel, and all angles are 90°.

2 Imagine 3-D shapes from 2-D drawings.

3 Recognise reflective symmetry in regular shapes.

▶ A mirror line can show reflective symmetry.

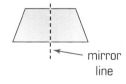

mirror line

Check out

1 Which of these shapes are rectangles? Give reasons for your answers.

a

b

c

2 Which one of these nets folds to make an open box?

a

b

c

3 Which of these letters have reflective symmetry?

A B
C D
E F
G H

2-D shape
S5.2

A 2-D shape is a flat shape.

3-D shape
S5.3

A 3-D shape is a solid.

add, addition
A1.5, N1.3, N1.4, N1.5, A2.2

Addition is the sum of two numbers or quantities.

altogether
A4.1

Altogether means 'in total'.

am, pm
S2.1

Before midday times are am, after midday they are pm.

analogue
S2.1

Analogue clocks have a face with hands and numbers

angle: acute, obtuse, right, reflex
S3.1, S3.2, S3.3, S3.4, S4.5, S5.1

An angle is formed when two straight lines cross or meet each other at a point. The size of an angle is measured in degrees (°).

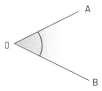

An acute angle is less than 90°.

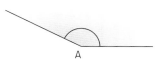

An obtuse angle is more than 90° but less than 180°.

A right angle is a quarter of a turn, or 90°.

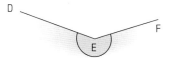

A reflex angle is more than 180° but less than 360°.

anticlockwise
S3.1, S3.3, S4.5, S4.6

Anticlockwise movement is the opposite way to the hands of a clock.

approximate, approximately
N5.2, N5.4

An approximate value is close to the actual value of a number.

area: square millimetre, square centimetre, square metre, square kilometre
A4.4, N5.1, S1.3, S1.4

The area of a surface is a measure of its size. Area is measured in units squared
For example, mm^2, cm^2, m^2, km^2.

axis, axes
A3.6, A5.8

An axis is one of the lines used to locate a point on a grid using coordinates.

balance
A4.3

An equation balances when the value is the same on both sides of the equals sign.

bar chart
D2.5, D3.3, D3.5

A bar chart is a diagram that uses rectangles of equal width to display data. The frequency is given by the height of the rectangle.

bar-line graph
D3.3

A bar-line graph is a diagram that uses lines to display data. The lengths of the lines are proportional to the frequencies.

brackets
S2.2

Operations in brackets should be done first.

calculate, calculation
N1.4, N3.2, A5.5

Calculate means work out.

calculator
N1.6

You can use a calculator to do calculations.

Carroll diagram
D2.1, D2.2

A Carroll diagram is used for sorting.

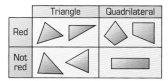

centimetre
A4.1, N5.1

A centimetre is a measure of short lengths.

certain
D1.4, D1.6, D4.1

An event which is certain will definitely happen.

chance
D1.4, D1.5, D4.1, D4.2

Chance is the probability of something happening.

check
A4.4

You check an answer to make sure it is correct.

circle
D1.1, D2.1

A circle is a perfectly round shape

clock
S2.1

A clock is used to tell the time.

clockwise
S3.1, S3.3, S4.5, S4.6

Clockwise movement is the same way
as the hands of a clock.

collect
D3.1

Collect means 'gather'.

compare
N2.4, N4.5

Compare means to look at similar and different aspects of things.

compass
S3.1

A compass points to a specific direction.

convert
N3.5

Convert means to change.

coordinates
S2.2, S2.3, A3.5, A3.6, S4.3, A5.6, A5.7, A5.8

Coordinates are the numbers that make up a coordinate pair. They describe the position of a point on a grid.

count, count on
D2.3, D3.1, A.4.4

You count by listing numbers in order. For example, 1, 2, 3, 4, ...

cube
S5.3

A cube is a 3-D square. All the sides are the same length.

cuboid
S5.3

A cuboid is a 3-D rectangle

data
D1.1, D1.2, D1.3, D2.4, D3.4

Data are pieces of information.

decimals, decimal fraction
N1.1, N2.4, N2.5, N3.3, N4.2, N4.3

A decimal fraction shows part of a whole represented as tenths, hundredths, thousandths and so on.
For example, 0.65 and 0.3 are decimal fractions.

decrease
N1.2, N1.3

Decrease means make less.

decimal point
N3.3

A decimal point separates the whole number part from the decimal point.

degree (°)
S3.1, S3.2, S4.5, S5.1

A degree is a measure of turn. There are 360° in a full turn.

denominator
N2.1, N2.2, N4.1, N4.3, N5.7

The denominator is the bottom number in a fraction. It shows how many parts the whole has been divided into.

$\frac{1}{2}$ ←— denominator

diagram
D3.2, D3.5, A5.5

A diagram is a line drawing that represents a situation.

difference
A1.3

You find the difference between two amounts by subtracting one from the other.

digit
N1.1, N1.6, N2.6

A digit is any of the numbers 0, 1, 2, 3, 4, 5, 6, 7, 8, 9.

digital
S2.1

A digital clock shows the time in numbers.

dimensions
S5.2, S5.3

The dimensions of an object are its measurements.

direction
S3.1

A direction is the way you go. For example, North.

display
D2.4

You can display or show lots of data in a graph or table.

distance
S1.2, S3.5, S4.3, S4.6

The distance between two points is the length of the line that joins them.

divide, division
A1.5, N2.1, N2.2, N2.3, N2.6, N3.4, N3.5, N3.7, N3.8, N4.1, N4.4, N5.5, N5.6, N5.7

Divide (÷) means share equally.
$6 ÷ 2 = 3$

double, halve
A3.1, A3.4, N2.3, N3.2, N3.8

To double means to multiply by 2. To halve is to divide by 2.

edge (of solid)
S1.2, S1.4, S5.2

An edge is a line along which two faces of a solid meet.

edge

equal (sides, angles)
S5.2, S5.4

Equal sides are the same length. Equal angles are the same size.

equal chance
D1.4, D1.6

Equal chance means that either choice is equally likely.

equal part
N4.1

Equal parts are the same size.

equal, equals (=)
N2.1, N2.4, N2.5, N2.6, S3.4,
S3.5, A4.2, A4.3, A4.4

Equal means having exactly the same value or size.

equally likely
D1.3

Events are equally likely if they have the same probability.

equation
A4.4, A5.1

An equation is a statement linking two expressions that have the same value.

equivalent, equivalence
N5.6

Equivalent fractions have the same value.

estimate
N2.4, N5.1, A3.5, S5.1

An estimate is an approximate answer.

even
A1.4

The even numbers are 2, 4, 6, 8, ...

even chance
D4.1

Even chance means that either choice is equally likely.

experiment
D4.2, D4.3

An experiment is a test or investigation to gather evidence for or against a suggestion.

expression
A2.2, A2.3

An expression is a collection of numbers and symbols linked by operations but not including an equals sign.

face
S2.5, S4.4

A face is a flat surface of a solid.

face

factor
A3.1, A3.2, N5.3

A factor is a number that divides exactly into another number. For example, 3 and 7 are factors of 21.

fair shares
N2.1

Equal shares are fair shares.

formula, formulas
A5.2, A5.3, A5.7

A formula is used to calculate a quantity.

fraction
N2.1, N2.2, N2.4, N2.5, N4.1, N4.2
N4.3, N5.5, N5.7, N5.8, D4.2

A fraction is a way of describing a part of a whole.
For example, $\frac{2}{5}$ of this shape is shaded.

frequency
D2.3, D3.4

Frequency is the number of times something occurs.

frequency table
D3.1, D4.2

A frequency table is a neat way of listing the frequency of different events.

Pet	Frequency
Dog	9
Cat	3

Glossary

frequent
D4.2

Frequent means 'often'.

full turn
S5.5

A full turn is 360°.

graph
A3.5, A3.6, A5.7

A graph shows the link between different data.

greater than (>)
A4.3

Greater than means more than. For example 4 > 3.

grid
S2.2, S2.3, S5.6, A3.5, A3.6, N5.4

A grid is a square pattern used to plot coordinate points.

group
N2.6, A2.2

You can group terms together if they are the same. For example, $x + x = 2x$.

half, halve
N2.3, N3.8, N5.6, N5.7, S3.1, S5.1, S5.4, A3.1

To halve is to divide by 2.

halfway
N3.1

Halfway is exactly in the middle.

height, high
A3.4, A3.5

Height is the vertical distance from the bottom to the top of a shape.

highest
N1.6, D3.5

Highest mean 'greatest'.

horizontal
D3.3

Horizontal means flat and level with the ground.

hundred
N2.5

One hundred is $10 \times 10 = 100$.

hundreds, tens, units, tenths, hundredths
N1.1, N1.6, N2.6, N3.1, N3.3, N3.4, N3.6, N4.2

Hundred = 100
Ten = 10
Unit = 1
Tenth = 0.1 or $\frac{1}{10}$
Hundredth = 0.01 or $\frac{1}{100}$

identical
N2.1

Identical means 'exactly the same'.

image
S4.2

When a shape is reflected, translated or rotated, the new shape is called the image.

mirror
original · image

impossible
D1.4, D1.6, D4.1

An event is impossible if it definitely cannot happen.

increase
A1.1, A5.4, N1.2, N1.3, N5.8

Increase means to make greater.

inequality
A4.3

An inequality is an expression where the two sides are not exactly equal.

input
A1.6

Input is data put into a machine or process.

interpret
D3.5

You interpret data whenever you make sense of it.

intersect, intersection
S3.5

Two lines intersect at the point where they cross. This is the intersection of the lines.

intersection

interval
N1.1

An interval is the size of a class or group in a frequency table.

inverse
A4.2, A5.1

An inverse operation undoes the original operation. For example, multiplication is the inverse of division.

jottings
N3.6, N5.5

Jottings are rough notes.

key
D2.4, D2.5, D3.2

A key explains what something means.

length: millimetre, centimetre, metre, kilometre; mile, foot, inch
S1.3, S1.4, S3.5, N5.1

Length is a measure of distance. It is often used to describe one dimension of a shape.
One kilometre = 1000 metres
One metre = 100 centimetres
One centimetre = 10 millimetres

less than (<)
A4.3

Less than means smaller than.
For example, 3 is less than 4, or 3 < 4.

letter
A4.1, A4.4

Letters (a–z or A–Z) are used to stand for unknown numbers in algebra.

like
A2.2

Like terms can be added together. For example, $2a$ and $6a$ are like terms. $2a + 6a = 8a$.

likelihood
D4.1

Likelihood is the probability of an event happening.

likely
D1.4, D1.6, D4.1

An event is likely if it will happen more often than not.

limit
N3.1

To round a number you look at the limits of the estimate.
For example, 6.55 rounds to 7 to the nearest whole number, as the limits are 6.50–7.49.

line
S2.2, S3.4

A line joins two points.

line of symmetry
S4.1, S5.4

You can fold a 2-D shape along a line of symmetry so that one half of the shape fits exactly on the other half.

machine
A1.6

A machine links an input value to an output value.

mapping
A3.4, A3.5, A3.6, A5.3, A5.5, A5.6, A5.7

A mapping is a rule that can be applied to a set of numbers to give another set of numbers.

mean
D1.3

The mean is an average value found by adding all the values and dividing by the number of values.

measure
S1.1, S3.2, S3.3, N2.4, N5.1

When you measure something you find the size of it.

median
D1.2

The median is an average which is the middle value when the data is arranged in size order.

1 2 3 (6) 9 12 13

The median of these numbers is 6.

minus
N1.2

Minus means 'subtract' or 'take away'.

mirror line
S4.2, S4.3, S4.6

A mirror line is a line or axis of symmetry.

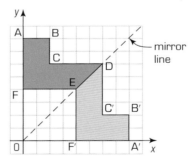

mode, modal
D1.1, D3.4

The mode is an average that is the data value that occurs most often.

1 1 (2 2 2) 3 4 5

The mode of these numbers is 2.

movement
S4.4

A shape has movement when it moves on a grid.

multiple
D2.2, A3.2

A multiple of a whole number is the product of that number and any other. For example, these are multiples of 6: $6 \times 4 = 24$ and $6 \times 12 = 72$.

multiply, multiplication
A1.5, A1.6, A3.1, A3.2, A3.4, N1.6
N2.3, N3.2, N3.6, N5.3, N5.4, N5.5,
A5.2, S1.3

Multiplication is combining two numbers to form a product. For example, $6 \times 3 = 15$.

nearest
N3.1

Nearest means the closest value.

negative
N1.2, N1.3, A5.8

A negative number is less than zero.

net
S5.3

A net is a 2-D diagram that can be folded to form a solid shape.

number line
N1.4

A number line shows numbers in order.

0   1   2   3   4

numerator
N2.1, N4.1, N5.7

The numerator is the top number in a fraction. It shows how many parts you are dealing with.

$\frac{3}{4}$ ← numerator

object
S4.2, S4.3

The object is the original shape before a transformation.

odd
A1.4

The odd numbers are 1, 3, 5, 7, ...

of
N2.3

'Of' means 'multiply'. For example, $\frac{1}{2}$ of $12 = \frac{1}{2} \times 12 = 6$.

operation
A1.5, A1.6, A4.2

An operation is a rule for numbers or objects.
The main operations are addition, subtraction, multiplication and division.

opposite
A1.5, S3.5, S5.2

Opposite means across from.

These pentagons are opposite each other.

order
A1.2, D1.2

To order means to arrange according to size or importance.

outcome
D4.1, D4.2, D4.3

An outcome is the result of a trial.

output
A1.6

Output is the answer produced by a machine or process.

overlap
D2.1

Two shapes overlap if they cross over each other.

pair
N1.4

A pair of numbers is two numbers.

parallel
S3.5, S5.2

Two lines that always stay the same distance apart are parallel. Parallel lines never cross or meet.

Glossary

partition, part
N2.1, N2.2, N3.6, N5.4

To partition means to split a number into smaller amounts, or parts. For example, 57 could be split into 50 + 7, or 40 + 17.

pattern
A1.1, A5.3, A5.4, A5.5, A5.6, S2.3

A pattern repeats itself.

percent, percentage (%)
N2.5, N4.3, N4.4, N5.8

A percentage is a fraction expressed as the number of parts per hundred.

perimeter
S1.2, S1.4, A2.3

The perimeter of a shape is the distance around it. It is the total length of the edges.

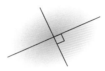

The perimeter of this rectangle is:
1 + 2 + 1 + 2 = 6.

perpendicular
S3.5

Two lines are perpendicular to each other if they meet at a right angle.

pictogram
D2.4, D2.5, D3.2

A pictogram is used to show data.

People at lunch

		☺ = 1 person
Girls	☺ ☺ ☺ ☺	
Boys	☺ ☺ ☺	
	Number	

place value
N1.1, N1.6, N3.3, N3.4, N3.5, N5.4

The place value is the value of a digit in a number. For example, in 3.65 the digit 6 has a value of 6 tenths.

plot
A3.6

Points are plotted on a grid.

point
S2.2, S2.3, S4.3, S4.4

A point is a fixed place on a grid or on a shape.

position
S2.2, S5.5

A position is a place or location.

positive
N1.2, N1.3

A positive number is greater than zero.

prism
S5.3

A prism is a 3-D shape that has the same shape all the way through.

This is a triangular prism.

probability
D1.6, D4.1, D4.2, D4.3

Probability is a measure of how likely an event is.

product
N5.3

A product is the result of a multiplication.

protractor
S3.3, S3.4

A protractor is an instrument for measuring angles in degrees.

pyramid
S5.3

A pyramid has a square or triangular base and triangular sides.

quadrant
A5.8

A coordinate grid is divided into four quadrants by the *x*- and *y*-axes.

quadrilateral: kite, parallelogram, rectangle, rhombus, square, trapezium
D2.1, S3.5, S5.2, N5.6, N5.7

A quadrilateral is a shape with four sides.

Rectangle

Parallelogram

Kite

All angles are right angles. Opposite sides equal.

Two pairs of parallel sides.

Two pairs of adjacent sides equal.

Rhombus

Square

Trapezium

All sides the same length. Opposite angles equal.

All sides and angles equal.

One pair of parallel sides.

quarter
S3.1, S5.1, N5.6, N5.7

A quarter is one fourth $\frac{1}{4}$.

ratio
N4.5

Ratio compares the size of one part with the size of another part.

rectangle
S1.2, S1.3, S1.4, S2.3, N2.2, N5.3

See quadrilateral.

reduce
N5.8

To reduce is to make smaller.

reflect, reflection
S4.1, S4.2, S4.3, S4.6, S5.6

A reflection is a transformation where the object and the image are the same distance from a mirror line.

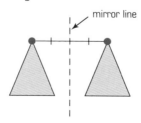

mirror line

regular
S5.4

A regular shape has equal sides and equal angles.

relationship
A3.4

A relationship is a link between objects or numbers.

repeat
A1.1

To repeat a pattern is to draw it again.

represent
A2.1, D2.4, D2.5

You can represent a number or quantity by a letter.

results
D3.1, D4.3

The results of a trial are a summary of the outcomes

right angle
S3.1, S3.2, S3.5, S5.1

A right angle is 90°.

rotate, rotation
S4.5, S4.6, S5.5

A rotation is a transformation where every point in the object turns through the same angle relative to a fixed point.

rotation symmetry
S5.5

A shape has rotation symmetry if when turned it fits onto itself more than once in a full turn.

round, rounding
N3.1

You round a number by writing it to a given accuracy.
For example, 639 is 600 to the nearest 100 and 640 to the nearest 10.
To round to one decimal place means to round to the nearest tenth.
For example 12.47 is 12.5 to 1 decimal place (dp).

row
A3.1

A row is a horizontal line that goes across a grid or table.

rule
A1.2, A1.3, A1.4, A5.4, A5.5, A5.6

A rule describes the link between objects or numbers.
For example, the rule linking 2 and 6 may be +4 or ×3.

ruler
S1.1

A ruler is an instrument for measuring lengths.

scale
S1.1, S3.3, S3.4, N2.4, D2.5, D3.3

A scale is a numbered line or dial.
The numbers usually increase in sequence.

sequence
A1.1, A1.2, A1.3, A1.4, A5.4

A sequence is a set of numbers or objects that follow a rule.
For example 1, 4, 8, 11, 14, ... (+3)

shape
S1.2, S4.3, S4.4, S4.6, S5.4

A shape is made by a line or lines drawn on a surface, or by putting surfaces together.

share
N4.1

Share means divide 'equally'.

side (of 2-D shape)
S3.4, S3.5

A side is a flat part of a shape.

← side

sort
D2.1, D2.2

Sort means 'put in order'.

square
S1.3, S2.2, S5.3, N2.2, D1.1

A four sided shape with equal angles and sides. See quadrilateral.

square number
A3.3

If you multiply a number by itself the result is a square number. For example, 25 is a square number because $5^2 = 5 \times 5 = 25$.

straight line
A3.6, S3.2, A5.7, S5.1

A straight line is the shortest distance between two points.

straight line

subtract, subtraction
A1.5, A2.2, A4.4, N1.3, N1.5, N3.8, N5.5

Subtraction is the operation that finds the difference in size between two numbers.
For example, $12 - 3 = 9$.

surface, surface area
S1.3, S1.4

The surface area of a solid is the total area of its faces.

survey
D1.2, D2.4, D2.5, D3.2

A survey is an investigation to find information.

symbol
A2.1, A2.2, A2.3, A5.3

You can use symbols to represent numbers.

symmetry, symmetrical
S4.1, S5.4

A shape is symmetrical if you can fold it exactly onto itself.

table
D2.2, D2.3

A table is an arrangement of information, numbers or letters usually in rows and columns.

take away
A1.5

Take away means 'subtract'.

tally
D2.3, D4.2

You use a tally mark to represent an object when you collect data. Tally marks are usually made in groups of five to make it easier to count them.

tally chart
D3.1

A tally chart is used to collect data.

Food	Tally
Cheese	︁︁﬩﬩ ﬩﬩

temperature
N1.2

Temperature is a measure c
It can be measured in degre

tenth
N2.4, N2.6, N4.2, N4.4

A tenth is 1 out of 10 or $\frac{1}{10}$.
For example, 0.5 has 5 tenths.

term
A1.3

A term is a number or object in a
It is also part of an expression.

turn
S3.1, S3.2, S4.5,

tessellate
S5.6

Shapes tessellate if they fit together without any gaps.

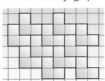

time
S2.1

Time is a measure of duration.
There are:
► 60 seconds in a minute
► 60 minutes in an hour
► 24 hours in a day
► 7 days in a week
► 28–31 days in a month
► 365 days in most years.

times table
N2.3, A3.1

A times table gives the multiples of a number.

total
D1.3

The total is the result of an addition.

translate, translation
S4.4, S4.6, S5.6

A translation is a transformation where an object moves a distance and direction. It is a sliding movement.

trial
D4.3

Each result of an experiment is called a trial.

triangle: equilateral, isosceles, scalene, right-angled
S2.3, S3.4, S5.2, S5.4, D1.1, D2.1

A triangle is a shape with three sides.

Equilateral

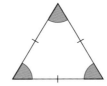

Three equal sides

Isosceles

Two equal sides

Scalene

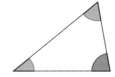

No equal sides

Right-angled

One angle is 90°

A turn is a rotation.

S4.6, S5.1, S5.5

units: metre, millimetre, centimetre, kilometre, tonne
N1.6, S1.1, S1.2, N3.5, N5.2

You measure a quantity in units.

unknown
A2.1, A4.1, A4.4

An unknown is a variable. You can often find it by solving an equation.

unlikely
D1.4, D1.6, D4.1

An unlikely event has a small chance of occuring.

value
A2.4, A3.5, A3.6, A4.3, A4.4, S2.2

The value is the amount an expression or variable is worth.

Venn diagram
D2.1, D2.2

Venn diagrams are used for sorting.

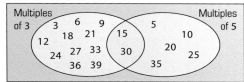

Numbers below 40

vertex, vertices
S5.3

A vertex of a shape is a point at which two or more edges meet.

vertical
D3.3

Vertical means straight up or down.

wage
A5.2

A wage is the money you earn for doing a job.

whole
N2.2, N2.5

The whole of a shape means all of it.

width
S1.3

Width is a measure of an object that describes how wide it is.

width

length

zero
N1.2

Zero is another name for 0 or nought.

A1 Check in

1 a 2, 5, 8, 11, 14, 17
  b 30, 26, 22, 18, 14, 10
2 9 25
3 a 12
  b 3
  c 9
  d 13
  e 20
  f 16

A1 Check out

1 a 30, 33
  b 15, 19, 23, 27, 31, 34, 37, 41
    The rule is +4.
2 a 21
    36
    48
  b 7
    4
    6
  c 210
    40
    480

N1 Check in

1 a Three hundred and seventy four
  b 423
2 a 17 23 26 35 41
  b 89 142 170 203 325
3 a 7
  b 4
  c 15

N1 Check out

1 a 70
  b 190
  c 280
  d 1430
2 ⁻4 °C ⁻3 °C 0 °C 1 °C 2 °C 5 °C
3 a 4 tenths
  b 5 units or ones
4 a 130
  b 60
  c 92
  d 43
  e 1200
  f 800
  g 496
  h 621

1 **a** yes
   b yes
   c no
   d no
   e no
   f no
2 **a** 2
   b 400 ml

1 **a** About 80 cm
   b About 15 cm or 150 mm
2 12 cm
3 15 cm^2

1 **a** 6 cubes
   b 3 cubes
2 **a** 6 squares shaded

   b 4 squares shaded

   c 3 squares shaded

1 **a** 6
   b 70
   c 400
2 **a** 0.6
   b 23.7
3 **a** $\frac{50}{100} = \frac{1}{2}$
      $\frac{75}{100} = \frac{3}{4}$
      $\frac{90}{100} = \frac{9}{10}$
   b 0.3   0.7   0.25

D1 Check in

1 **a** 1 2 3 4 5

b 3 7 8 9 11

c 1 2 3 4 5 7

d 2 4 6 7 8 12

2 **a** $\frac{1}{4}$

b $\frac{1}{3}$

c $\frac{1}{5}$

D1 Check out

1 2 3 3 3 4 5 5 6

The mode is 3

2 **a** Certain

b Possible or Likely

c Impossible

d Possible

e Possible or Likely

A2 Check in

1 **a** $7 + 6 = 13$

b $12 + 8 = 20$

c $12 + 6 = 18$

2 **a** 10 cm

b 12 cm

A2 Check out

1 **a** 3 more than n

b 4 less than n

c Double or twice n

2 **a** $n + 3$ cars

b $n - 2$ pears

1 a 5 o'clock

b 2.20 or twenty past 2

2 a Right-angled triangle

b Rectangle

3 a 1, 3, 5, 7, 9

b 2, 5, 8, 11, 14

c 18, 14, 10, 6, 2

1

24-hour	12-hour
20:00	8 pm
10:45	10.45 am
18:15	6.15 pm
02:00	2 am
21:20	9.20 pm
11:30	11.30 am

2 A (3, 2)

B (1, 4)

C (5, 1)

D (2, 5)

1 a 3

b 8

c 13

2 5

1 a 40 people

b At 10 am

c At 4 pm

After school, so more families picking up books.

2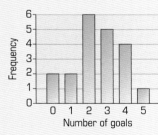

N3 Check in

1 a 20

b 70

c Either, but usually 40.

2 a 15

b 14

c 80

d 3

e 8

f 9

3 3 and 4

N3 Check out

1 For example, 3.45

2 a £40

b £60

c £100

d £140

e £180

3

	a	b
Aberdeen	700	660
Edinburgh	500	540
Fort William	700	650
Kendal	400	400
Leeds	400	380

4 a 2500 g or 2.5 kg

A 1 kg large potato is 4 times heavier

b £5 ÷ 19 = 26.3

26 bars

A3 Check in

1 20   5   25

2 A (2, 1)

B (3, 3)

C (4, 2)

3 a Rectangle

b Square

A3 Check out

1 8, 20, 32.

2 1 and 30, 2 and 15, 3 and 10, 5 and 6

3

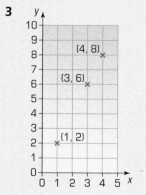

1 **a** 3
   b 2
2 **a** and **b**
   c is obtuse
   d is reflex

1 **a**, **d**, **b**, **c**
2

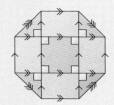

3 **a**, **d**

1 79   225   530   591   917
2 **a** D, **b** B, **c** C, **d** A

1 **a** 6
   b 9
   c 4
   d 5
2 **a** 0.3
   b 0.47
   c 0.62
3 **a** 0.15
   b 0.19
   c 0.52
   d 0.6
4 **a** £3
   b 100 g
   c £25

A4 Check in

1 a 31

 b 25

 c 55

 d 44

2 6   9   12   17   31

A4 Check out

1 a 7216 < 7261

 b 18 523 < 18 532

 c 23 > 17 + 5

 d 18 − 3 = 15

2 14 + 15 = 29   15 + 16 = 31

 The sum of two consecutive numbers is always odd.

3 a 70

 b 57

 c 13

S4 Check in

1 a Yes

 b Yes

 c No

 d No

2 a 360°

 b 90°

 c 180°

S4 Check out

1 a Yes

 b No

2

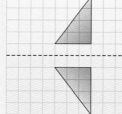

3 4 right then 2 down.

1 a 6
   b 15
   c 35
   d 24
   e 48
   f 56
   g 5
   h 9
   i 6
   j 3
   k 6
   l 8
2 a $\frac{1}{5}$
   b $\frac{1}{3}$
   c $\frac{1}{4}$

1 1 and 48, 2 and 24, 3 and 16, 4 and 12, 6 and 8.
2 3 kg   5 kg   14 kg   19 kg   7 kg   12 kg
3 a 350 g
   b 100 kg
   c £50
   d 40 litres
   e 34 cm
   f 20 m
4 a 108 eggs; 16 boxes
   b £7.80

1 a

Colour	Frequency
Blue	
Red	
Green	
Yellow	
Orange	

= 2 students

b

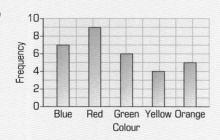

1

Score	Tally	Frequency
1	JHT IIII	9
2	JHT JHT	10
3	JHT III	8
4	JHT I	6
5	JHT IIII	9
6	JHT III	8

2

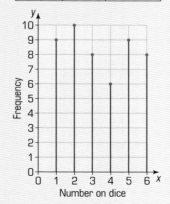

3 The modal score is 2.

It is the most common, and has the highest frequency.

D4 Check in

1 16   8   20

  a $\frac{3}{5}$

  b $\frac{1}{6}$

  c $\frac{2}{3}$

D4 Check out

1 For example, E C D B A   or   DEC   B A

2 **a** 3 students

  b 1 pet

  c $3 + 2 = 5$ students

  d $3 + 11 + 4 + 7 + 3 + 2 = 30$ students

A5 Check in

1 **a** $^-3\,°C$ $^-12\,°C$

  b $^-12\,°C$, $^-3\,°C$, $1\,°C$, $5\,°C$.

2

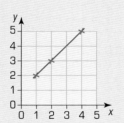

They make a straight line.

A5 Check out

1 The pattern number multiplied by itself (or squared.)

2 **a** 23, 34, 45, 56, 67.

  b 57, 49, 41, 33, 25, 17.

3

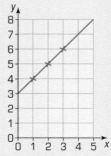

For example, (0, 3) or (4, 7).

1 **a** Yes
   b Yes
   d No
2 **a** 2
   b 1
   c None

1 **a** No. Only one set of opposite lines parallel, plus one side shorter than the other.
   b Yes. Both pairs of opposite sides equal and parallel, angles are 90°.
   c No. Opposite sides are equal and parallel but angles are not 90°.
2 B
3 A, B, C, D, E, H.

Index

A

acute angles, 134, 236
addition, 10, 162
   mental, 22
   with negatives, 20
   with symbols, 70–2
am, pm, 80
analogue clocks, 80
angles, 132–9, 174, 236
   acute and obtuse, 134
   drawing, 138
   equal, 238, 242
   measuring, 136
anticlockwise, 132, 136, 174, 176
approximations, 182, 187
area, 34–7
axes, 128, 232

B

bar charts, 96, 202, 206
bar line chart, 202
brackets, 82

C

calculations, 15–28, 179–196
calculators, 26
Carroll diagrams, 88–91
chance, 60–3, 210, 212
   see also probability
clocks, 80
clockwise, 132, 136, 174, 176
collecting data, 198
compasses, 132
converting: m, cm and mm, 108
coordinates
   of shapes, 84
   plotting, 126, 128, 170, 228, 230, 232
   reading, 82, 170

D

data, 87–98, 197–208
   collecting, 198
   displaying, 92, 94, 200, 202
   interpreting, 90, 96, 204–6
   mean, 58
   median, 56
   mode, 54, 204
   sorting, 88
decimals, 16, 46, 104
   and fractions, 46, 146, 148
   and percentages, 48, 148
degrees, 132, 134, 174, 236
denominators, 40, 42, 144, 148, 192
diagrams, 200, 226
   bar charts, 96, 202
   bar line graphs, 202
   Carroll diagrams, 88–91
   interpreting, 206
   pictograms, 94, 200
   sequences in, 8
   tally charts, 92, 198
   Venn diagrams, 88–91
digital clocks, 80
distance
   on a grid, 170, 176
   measuring, 32
division, 10, 106, 108, 112, 114
   and fractions, 42, 44, 144, 150, 191, 192
   and percentage, 150
   written method, 188

E

edges
   see perimeter
equal
   angles, 238, 242
   chance, 60, 64
   part, 144
   sides, 238, 242
equalities, 158
equations, 155–164
   checking results, 162
   solving, 218
   see also formulas
equivalent fractions, 190
estimating, 46–7, 126, 180
experiments and probability, 212–5

F

factors, 118, 120, 184
formulas, 220, 222, 230
fractions, 40–52, 144–50, 190–5, 212
   and decimals, 46, 48, 146, 148
   and percentages, 48, 148, 150, 194

comparing, 42
equivalent, 190
simplifying, 144
frequency, 92
frequency tables, 92, 198, 204, 212

G
graphs, 126, 128, 202, 228, 230
    see also diagrams
grids
    movement of shapes, 176
    plotting coordinates, 82, 84, 126, 128
    symmetry, 170
    translating shapes, 172

I
image, 168
inequalities, 160
input, 12
interpreting data, 204–6
inverse operations, 158, 218

J
jottings, 110, 188

K
keys, 94, 200

L
likelihood, 60, 64, 210
lines of symmetry, 166, 242

M
mapping, 124, 126, 128, 222, 226,
    228, 230
mean, 58
measuring
    angles, 134–7
    length, 30, 46, 180
median, 56
mental calculations, 22–25, 102
minus
    see negative numbers
mirror lines, 168, 170, 176
mode, 54, 204
multiples, 90, 120
multiplication, 10, 12, 26, 34, 118, 120,
    124, 184, 188, 220
    by partitioning, 110
    calculations, 186
    decimals, 104
    mental, 102, 220

N
negative numbers, 18, 20, 232
nets, of solid shapes, 240
number lines, 22
numerator, 40, 144, 192

O
obtuse angles, 134, 136, 236
operations, 10, 12, 158
ordering, 4, 56
outcomes, 210–5
output, 12

P
parallel lines, 140, 238
partitioning, 110, 186
patterns
    in coordinates, 84, 228
    in formulas, 222
    in sequences, 2, 224, 226
percentages, 150, 194
    and decimals, 48, 148
    and fractions, 148
    finding, 194
perimeters, 32, 36, 72
perpendicular lines, 140
pictograms, 94, 96, 200
place value, 16, 26, 104–8, 186
    hundreds, tens, units, tenths, hundredths, 16, 26,
    50, 100, 104, 106, 110, 146
probability, 64, 209–16
    describing, 210
protractors, using, 136–9

Q
quadrants, 232
quadrilaterals, 88, 140, 238

R
ratio, 152
rectangles
    area, 34, 36
    perimeters, 32, 36
reflection, 166–71, 176, 247
results, recording, 198, 214
right angles, 132, 134, 140, 236
rotation, 174, 176, 244
rotational symmetry, 244
rounding numbers, 100
rules
    graphs, 228
    sequences, 4–9, 224–9

Index

S

scales, 30
  decimals, 46
  charts and graphs, 96, 202
  protractors, 136–8
sequences, 1–14, 224
  patterns, 2, 224, 226
  rules, 4–9, 224–9
shapes
  2-D, 238
  3-D, solid, 240
  perimeters, 32
  symmetry, 170, 242
  transformations, 170–8
simplifying fractions, 144
sorting, 88, 90
square numbers, 122
squares, 242
straight lines, 128, 134, 230, 236
subtraction, 10, 162
  in division, 114, 188
  mental, 24
  with negatives, 20
  with symbols, 70
surface area, 34, 36
surveys, 56, 94, 96, 200
symbols, using, 67–78
symmetry, 166–171, 242, 244

T

tables, of data, 90–5, 198
tally charts, 92, 198, 212
temperature, 18
tenths, 46, 48, 146, 150
tessellation, 246
time, 80
times tables, 44, 118
transformations, 165–178
translation, 172, 176, 246
trial, 214
triangles, 138, 238, 242
turns, 132, 134, 174, 176, 236, 244

U

units: metre, millimetre, centimetre, kilometre, 26, 30, 32, 108
unknowns, 68, 156, 162

V

values
  coordinates, 82, 126, 128
  equations, 74, 160–2
  input and output, 12
Venn diagrams, 88, 90
vertices, 240

Z

zero, 18

×	1	2	3	4	5	6	7	8	9	10
1	1	2	3	4	5	6	7	8	9	10
2	2	4	6	8	10	12	14	16	18	20
3	3	6	9	12	15	18	21	24	27	30
4	4	8	12	16	20	24	28	32	36	40
5	5	10	15	20	25	30	35	40	45	50
6	6	12	18	24	30	36	42	48	54	60
7	7	14	21	28	35	42	49	56	63	70
8	8	16	24	32	40	48	56	64	72	80
9	9	18	27	36	45	54	63	72	81	90
10	10	20	30	40	50	60	70	80	90	100